Feed Your Vegetarian Teen

A practical guide to serving easy meals the whole family will enjoy

Donna P. Feldman, MS RDN

ISBN: **10:150246781X**
ISBN-**13:978-1502467812**

DEDICATION

To my mom, Gloria.
Thanks for the healthy start in life.

And to the clients and friends whose own experiences dealing with their vegetarian and vegan teenagers inspired me to write this book.

CONTENTS

Acknowledgments   i

1   Help! My kid wants to be a vegetarian!   3

2   Vegetarian Teen Basics   9

3   Protein from plants   16

4   Nutrition and the Meatless Teen   21

5   Less Meat – Better Environment   27

6   Shopping and Cooking Tips   33

7   Beans   42

8   Grains   70

9   Noodles   92

10   Potatoes and More   108

11   No Time to Cook – quick meal ideas   122

12   Summing It Up   124

13   References   126

14   Recipe Index   130

15   About the Author   132

ACKNOWLEDGMENTS

Many thanks to Susan McEachren and Nancy Sullivan for their wise advice about writing, formatting and publishing.

I'm very grateful for the encouragement and support and advice from my colleagues, including Kathy Isacks, MPS RD CDE and Constance Roark, MS RDN.

Finally, I must acknowledge all the wisdom about book writing and publishing that I've gotten over the past few years from various members of the Nutrition Entrepreneurs Authors dietetic practice group. I don't know many of them personally, but their shared expertise and experiences have been a great help.

Cover design by Sam Mestas: www.sammestas.com
Cover photos by Donna Feldman
Portraits by Rebekah West Photography: www.rebekahwest.com

HELP!
MY KID WANTS TO BE A VEGETARIAN!

What do you do when your child -- or spouse, partner, mom, dad or roommate -- announces "I'm giving up meat. I'm going to be a vegetarian." Or even more alarming, they're going to be a *vegan!* How do you shop, plan and cook? Will it be all about weird food, complicated recipes and food that doesn't taste good? Will everyone in the family have to give up meat too? Will it be healthy? What about protein and all the other nutrients people get from meat? And most important: will it taste good?

Take a deep breath. Stay calm. Having a new vegetarian or vegan in your family or circle of friends sounds like a big hassle. But don't worry. It's not and this book will help you. You'll find all the necessary guidance and recipes you need to avoid cooking two separate dinners every night. Everyone gets to eat foods they enjoy and meat eaters don't have to give up meat.

You'll also find information about nutrition for your vegetarian teen. And there's background on all the reasons eating less meat is a good idea for everyone.

The recipes in this book make meal preparation simple, even if you're feeding vegetarians, meat eaters and vegans at the same meal. Grains and grain products, beans and vegetables are the primary ingredients. By adding small amounts of high protein foods, like meat, fish, cheese, tofu, beans or nuts, one basic recipe can work for everybody. These are one-pot meals, which makes grocery shopping and cooking less complicated. Suggestions for easy side dishes are included, to add more variety and balance.

Even better: these recipes aren't fussy gourmet concoctions, requiring expensive exotic ingredients and complicated cooking techniques, leaving a big mess to clean up. It's all about basic food and putting a healthy dinner on the table that works for the whole family. I've been cooking this way for years. My goals for you are that after reading this book you'll feel more confident and less stressed, knowing that

* your vegetarian child is getting all the nutrients he or she needs

* you have the ability to put together easy meals that work for everyone

Who knows? You might even find that the dedicated meat eaters in the family enjoy meals that are more plant-based. And that can be good for everyone. Research consistently links a vegetarian diet with health benefits.

What do vegetarians eat? Or not eat?

- A classic vegetarian diet eliminates animal flesh: meat, poultry and fish.
- Some vegetarians do eat fish
- Vegetarians do eat milk, cheese, yogurt and eggs.

What do vegans eat? Or not eat?

- The vegan diet is much stricter. Vegans do not eat anything that comes from an animal: no meat, fish, eggs, dairy products.
- Some vegans also object to sauces (ex: fish sauce or Worcestershire) made with animal products.

A diet loaded with meat is linked to increased risk for heart disease, obesity, Type 2 diabetes, metabolic syndrome, inflammation and some cancers. The evidence linking lower meat intake to better health is now so overwhelming that the 2015 U.S. Dietary Guidelines includes this statement:

> *"..a healthy dietary pattern is higher in vegetables, fruits, whole grains, low- or non-fat dairy, seafood, legumes, and nuts;....lower in red and processed meats.."*

There are plenty of studies linking vegetarian and vegan diets to improved health and lower weight. Here are just a few examples (you can find the citations listed in the References):

'Beyond Meatless, the Health Effects of Vegan Diets'. Vegan diets protect against heart disease, some cancers, hypertension, Type 2 diabetes and cognitive function, while protecting against obesity.

'Vegetarian diet could slash blood pressure'. A meta-analysis of data from almost 40 studies shows that a vegetarian diet lowers blood pressure, and the effect is as strong as the effect of losing weight or cutting sodium intake.

'Predominantly Plant Diets Help Patients Shed Pounds.' Patients on vegan or vegetarian diets for 2 months lost more weight than patients eating typical meat-based diets. Even when the dieters were allowed to add back whatever foods they desired, the vegans and vegetarians continued losing more weight.

'Major habitual dietary patterns are associated with .. cardiovascular risk markers.' Low intake of fruit and vegetables and high consumption of red meat were associated with increased risk for heart disease.

'Nutrient profiles of vegetarian and nonvegetarian dietary patterns'. Meat eaters consume less fiber and more saturated fat and weighed more than vegetarians.

To be fair, some of the problems with a meat-heavy diet are caused by the lack of plant foods, not the meat itself. Meat-centric diets can end up being unbalanced. Result: a high protein/high saturated fat intake. Fiber and all the vitamins, minerals and antioxidants present in plant foods are lacking.

But it's not all bad news about meat and health. Some of the more significant nutritional contributions of animal foods are:

- meat, fish and poultry: iron, zinc, B12, choline
- Dairy foods: very high in calcium, B12, fortified with vitamin D
- Fatty fish: our only natural source of long chain omega-3 fatty acids, and if you eat fish livers, vitamin D
- Eggs: iron, choline

Vegans may have an especially hard time finding food sources of some of these nutrients.

There's another significant benefit of meat and dairy foods: they taste good. And for plenty of people, that's enough reason not to give them up.

The Take Away Message:

Meat doesn't have to be an all-or-nothing choice. You don't have to choose between eating meat *or* being a vegan. Just eat *less* meat. The recipes in this book use focus on vegetables and grains, with modest portions of protein foods. Result: more nutritional balance:

- high fiber - and a high variety of fiber
- high in vitamins and minerals,
- high in antioxidants
- adequate high quality protein
- low sugar
- few additives like flavorings, colorings, preservatives, texturizers
- naturally low in sodium
- modest amount of healthy fats
- less saturated fat and calories

HOW THIS BOOK IS ORGANIZED

The first 5 chapters are all about the *WHY* of eating less meat. There are several compelling reasons to cut back, ranging from health concerns to environmental concerns. I'm not trying to convince you to join your meatless teen. But you should be familiar with the basics. Your teen may already have some of this information.

The rest of the book is all about recipes. There are sections for different types of dishes, and all of the sections include ideas for side dishes to make the one-pot meals more balanced. Everyone likes variety, and while a one-dish meal may be just fine and very easy, there are lots of really simple no-fuss side dishes that enhance variety and nutritional balance. Especially important for teenagers who are growing and/or are active in sports.

VEGETARIAN TEEN BASICS

Vegetarian and vegan foods aren't new. In many parts of the world, meat is in short supply, and people are vegetarian by default. Our hunger-gatherer ancestors were vegetarian when they couldn't find animals to kill. Vegetarian cuisine is a tradition in India and other parts of Asia.

Lately, vegetarian and vegan diets get so much media coverage, you'd think half of us were avoiding meat. But according to a 2012 Gallup Poll, only about 5% of adults in the U.S. identified as vegetarian; 2% said they were vegan. These rates were essentially unchanged from the same survey done 10 years earlier. However, Gallup didn't survey teenagers. Meanwhile a 2015 survey by the Food Marketing Institute found that 7% of households reportedly had a vegetarian or vegan.

When I dove into vegetarian cooking years ago, it was a novel concept in the U.S. and other Western countries. There were no vegetarian convenience foods, few vegetarian restaurants or cookbooks and little information to go on. If you were avoiding meat, you were on your own. You were also rather weird. Vegetarianism was about rebellious '60's counter culture identity and rejection of middle class values. One of those rejected values was the emphasis on meat as a status symbol of a growing middle class.

But today cultural rebellion is over. Vegetarianism is mainstream and people usually adopt meatless eating for a specific reason:

- Health benefits
- Animal welfare
- Environmental concerns
- Cost
- Dislike of meat
- Peer pressure (especially common in teens)

In the past decades, nutrition science has added a wealth of information about the benefits of plant-based diets, from lower weight to longer life to fewer disease risks. But still, when a teen becomes vegetarian or vegan, parents worry about nutrition and health. Teens are growing, and animal foods provide high quality protein and other key nutrients. Parents want answers:

- Will she get enough protein? How will I know?
- Will I have to cook strange food? I don't have time to learn about that.
- Will I have to *eat* strange food?
- What other nutrients will be missing? Will a multiple vitamin make up for those?
- Will my child become unhealthy, or less fit?

There are as many ways to handle the situation as there are families. For example, one set of parents required their prospective vegetarian teen to research and write a report about the nutritional impact of vegetarianism. The report had to include a list alternative foods that would supply missing nutrients. Another teen was expected to plan her own meals and had responsibility for making sure the ingredients for those meals were on the shopping list. Another mom just sent her vegetarian daughter into the kitchen to make a PB & J sandwich if there were no meatless options at dinner.

What the best approach? Mom and Dad should *not* have to take on their teen's new meatless meal preferences as another chore. But they also should not leave their teen to fend for him/herself for food. Peanut butter sandwiches are fine, but they shouldn't be a dietary mainstay. That would be unbalanced, not to mention boring. Engage with your teen, so she participates in family meal decisions. Share mealtimes as often as your busy schedule permits, using the recipes in this book to make life easier and meal preparation simpler.

Eating disorders and vegetarian teens

While most teens, and adults, who give up meat do so for legitimate reasons, there is one potentially worrisome reason that a teen becomes vegetarian: a developing eating disorder. For some teens on the path to anorexia, a vegetarian diet is just one stop on the path to severe and irrational diet restrictions. The catch is how to tell the difference between a teen whose goal is to give up meat and the teen whose goal is to restrict food choices.

First, parents shouldn't assume giving up meat equals an eating disorder. Opposing a vegetarian diet because of unfounded fears will hurt your credibility. Instead, look for other warning signs of eating disorders. Giving up meat is rarely the only restriction. Typically the eating disordered teen is restricting all kinds of foods. He or she may quickly become vegan, giving up *all* animal products. She may restrict other foods or ingredients, like sugar or all fats or wheat or other major food groups. He may rationalize the restrictions by claiming to have allergies. And of course there will be other signs, including dramatic weight loss, cold body temperature, hair loss and depression. A child caught in the spiral of an eating disorder needs intervention from qualified medical providers. If your vegetarian child quickly progresses to being vegan, to pushing food around his plate, not eating and losing weight, it's time to act.

Engage your teen with meal preparation and share family meals. Leaving a newly-vegetarian or vegan teen to figure out his or her own food choices and meals is isolating. Stay aware of what your teen is really eating. If you observe worrisome behaviors or signs, contact your child's pediatrician. You will find other helpful online resources about eating disorders in the References section, on page 127.

Will my overweight teen lose weight?

A vegetarian diet doesn't automatically cause weight loss. Weight is about calories eaten and calories burned by activity. But plenty of people do lose weight on vegetarian diets, and on vegan diets. Cutting meat and dairy foods from the diet means rethinking all food choices. If your teen's diet was heavy on pizza and fast food, the restrictions of a vegan/vegetarian diet may lead to an overall reduction in food intake.

The good news would be that your teen starts eating more plant-based foods like vegetables, grains, nuts and fruit. Higher intake of those foods is linked to lower body weight.

The bad news would be that your teen simply switches to high calorie junk food and treats that don't include meat or dairy ingredients. Soft drinks, chips, pastries, cookies, energy bars and sugary cereals may be free of meat and dairy. That doesn't make them healthy.

If your teen is starting a vegetarian diet as a weight loss strategy, you may need to investigate where that decision came from. If it came from a friend who has an eating disorder (see above), you will need to pay attention to your own child's food choices, so the weight loss diet doesn't spiral into something else. If your teen made the decision on his/her own, it might be a good opportunity to discuss and implement healthier diet choices. If the vegetarian diet leads to lower intake of junk food and sugar, and more intake of plant-based foods, then great! Weight loss may be one result.

What if your prospective vegetarian is 6 yrs. old?

What if your elementary-aged child announces she or he wants to be a vegetarian. It's happening more frequently. What to do?

First, a child this young is not in a position to dictate family food choices. You need to ask some questions about where this idea came from: a friend at school? A TV character? A relative? The source of the idea may dictate how you deal with the request.

Second, you need to figure out if your young child even knows what "vegetarian" means. Does it just sound cool for some reason, because a popular friend or celebrity claims to be vegetarian?

Do a reality check. Does your wannabe vegetarian love hamburgers or chicken or turkey sandwiches or hotdogs? Clearly going vegetarian is going to interfere with those foods. You might point that out. Or not.

If you want to support your child's intent, you could come up with a plan to be a part-time vegetarian (and this book can help!), serving up more meatless meals, or serving meals that have flexible protein sources.

Young children don't need to know all the details of nutritional science. The best approach is to describe healthy foods as just that: "Healthy". They help you grow and have energy and be strong. For example, rather than focusing on protein, you can describe meat or milk or tofu or beans as foods that help muscles grow.

Plenty of kids grow up vegetarian. It's easy to create healthy balanced vegetarian diets for young children. Milk, yogurt and cheese are excellent sources of protein and calcium, both critical for growth.

Bottom Line: if your young child expresses an interest in being vegetarian, ask questions in a non-judgmental way and find out where the idea came from. Be flexible. It might be a short-lived idea and the sight (and smell) of one delicious hamburger puts the vegetarian diet on the back burner.

What if my "vegetarian" teen eats chicken, fish or turkey?

Some kids who claim to be vegetarians do still eat these foods. Poultry and fish are not vegetarian, strictly speaking, so this doesn't seem to make any sense. Basically, the definition of vegetarian becomes "no red meat".

What to do? Go with the flow. Unless your whole family is vegetarian, and you object to these foods, let them define vegetarian however they want. Nagging wouldn't be helpful. And it will make your life easier in terms of food choices.

Summing it up

Truthfully, feeding a vegetarian teen will be easier than feeding a vegan teen. You'll have more food choices (eggs, dairy foods), so the diet can be more varied. It's much easier to eat enough protein when you include cheese, milk, yogurt and eggs in your diet. Plus other key nutrients, like B12 and calcium, are more likely to be covered. And it's easier to get the rest of the family on board with many familiar vegetarian/meatless dishes, such as mac and cheese or bean burritos. Who doesn't like those?

Feeding a vegan teen requires more effort, but as time goes on, it will become easier. Be flexible, but don't let your teen slack off and live on processed soy burgers. Eventually your vegan teen may become a vegan adult, responsible for his or her own food decisions. Learning how to compose a healthy and varied vegan diet will be a very important life lesson.

Finally, your adventure with a vegetarian or vegan diet may be short lived. Teens may dive into a project like meatless eating, and then move on to some other project, eating meat occasionally.

PROTEIN FROM PLANTS

When a child announces her intention to be a vegetarian or vegan, the first thing that comes to mind for a parent is: "What about protein?" Because most people understand these protein basics:

- meat and animal foods like milk and cheese are high protein.
- protein is important.

What people *don't* realize is that many plant foods contain high quality protein. Knowing which foods those are is a key part of smart meatless meals.

PROTEIN PRIMER

Protein is the most important structural component of our cells. Cell membranes and internal cell structures require protein. Proteins are essential parts of hormones and transport molecules. Every muscle system, from the heart to digestion to skeletal muscles, depends on protein. It's also a structural component in bone and cartilage.

What exactly are proteins? They're long chains of unique molecules called amino acids. There are 22 different amino acids in the human body. Eight of them are essential, meaning humans cannot synthesize them. Those essential amino acids (EAA) 8 *must be consumed from food*.

Since protein chains vary in length, and there are 22 amino acids to use to make the chains, the possibilities for amino acid sequences are endless. These amino acid chains don't just float around like long strings. The protein chains twist and fold and kink into lumps, depending on which amino acids are where in the chain. Each protein ends up with a unique shape, critical to its unique function.

Not only do we need to consume all 8 essential amino acids, we need to eat specific *ratios* of those eight, to meet our protein needs. The protein quality of a food depends on the ratios and amounts of those essential amino acids in that food. Protein quality scoring methods have been devised over past decades to identify high quality protein sources. The Protein Digestibility Corrected Amino Acid Score (or PDCAAS) has been used for many years. The score is based strictly on amino acid content of the food. You can see from the chart that milk, egg and soy protein are considered very high quality, while grains are lower quality.

But the protein in some foods is more digestible and bioavailable than others. In 2013, the Food and Agriculture Organization of the UN proposed that a new method be used: the Digestible Indispensable Amino Acid Score (or DIAAS). This quality scoring system takes protein digestibility and bioavailability more into account. For example, soy protein is not rated so high by the DIAAS system compared to the PDCAAS method, because soy is less fully digestible.

PDCAAS-score of protein quality
1 is high quality; 0 is lowest
1.00 cow milk, whey, egg, soy protein
0.92 beef
0.91 soy beans
0.78 chickpeas
0.76 fruit
0.73 vegetables
0.70 legumes
0.59 cereal grains
0.52 peanuts
0.42 whole wheat

Now you know more than you ever wanted to know about protein quality scoring systems and their alphabet soup, tongue twisting names. Regardless of what system you use, protein from animal foods is considered to be high quality. The amino acid ratios closely resemble human requirements, and the protein in these foods is highly bioavailable. This just makes sense. Genetically, humans are more closely related to animals than to grasses or bean plants. Animals have muscles; those muscles are what we eat as meat.

Plants do not have muscles. Nevertheless, plants do contain protein. But the ratios of essential amino acids in plant proteins do not match the requirement of humans very well. Typically one or more of the 8 essential amino acids is lacking. Grains, like wheat, lack lysine. Beans, like kidney beans, lack methionine.

For example, because lysine is lacking in wheat, a person who tried to get all her protein just from wheat would have to eat a lot of wheat in order to consume enough lysine. But when beans *and* wheat are combined in the diet, the amino acid pattern more closely corresponds to the ideal pattern for humans. The lower lysine content of wheat is improved by the higher lysine content of beans. The higher proportion of methionine in wheat complements the lower level in the beans. Result: higher quality protein.

The way to improve the quality of plant proteins is to combine different plant foods. It's easier to get higher quality protein from a dish that combines grains *and* beans, than from a dish that contains only grains, or only beans. The plant proteins *complement* each other. They make up for each other's amino acid deficiencies. It's a plant protein marriage made in protein quality heaven.

The book *"Diet for a Small Planet"*, by Frances Moore Lappé, was the original blueprint for creating vegetarian dishes with higher quality protein by combining plant foods. She turned existing information about human protein requirements into recipes, based on the idea of complementary food proteins.

'Diet for a Small Planet' was first published in the late 1960's. Despite the focus on grains and beans, the recipes made liberal use of cheese, eggs and milk to boost the protein content of recipes. While this was still technically meatless, the cultural fixation with protein remained. No meat? No problem. High protein cheese, eggs and dairy are excellent protein sources too.

Since then, nutrition experts have taken a more flexible approach to the science of complementary plant proteins. We don't need to eat exact amounts of complementary plant protein foods at each meal. Eating a balanced and varied vegetarian diet over the course of a day or week should provide the right balance. The key is balance and variety. It's not practical to get all your protein from one type of plant food, whether grains or beans or nuts.

How much protein do we *need* everyday?

Recommended protein intake and protein content of foods, are listed in grams of total protein. The individual amino acids are not listed separately, nor are the EAAs listed separately.

The standard method used to determine the recommended minimum daily protein intake for an adult is 0.8 grams of protein per kilogram of body weight (or .56 grams per pound of body weight). According to this method, an average adult woman needs only about 46 grams of protein/day, while a man needs 56.

Unfortunately this calculation does not tell us what an *optimal* protein intake might be. The daily protein requirement varies according to age, gender and height. Athletes may need proportionally more protein to build muscle. There is growing evidence that adults 60 years and older may need a higher protein intake to prevent muscle loss. People recovering from illness or injury may need more protein, as do pregnant or lactating women.

Growing children, including teens, need proportionally more grams of protein per pound of body weight to support healthy growth. While an infant might only consume 10 grams of protein per day, that represents 1 gram per pound for a 10 pound baby, almost twice the recommendation for an adult.

According to the CDC, the minimum daily protein intake for average teens is 46 grams for girls and 52 grams for boys.

For a more individualized calculation, try this handy University of Maryland Medical System protein calculator:
www.healthcalculators.org/calculators/protein.asp
According to this calculator, a 6-foot, 150 lb. 15 year old boy who participates in active sports needs twice the minimum recommendation.

Keep in mind: most people, even vegetarians, already eat more than the minimum for protein everyday. So while the minimum recommendations are interesting, they may not mean much to people in the real world.

Eating is not a math problem

With all the talk about grams of protein and calculations of recommended intake, it's easy to start thinking healthy eating is a major math problem. How much do you need to worry about accuracy when it comes to your teen's protein intake?

Answer: not so much. First of all, unless you or your teen are living in a locked diet research ward, where every molecule of food you eat, or don't eat, is weighed and measured before and after your meal, 100% accuracy is impossible. Even nutrition facts labels on food products are permitted to vary by a certain percentage. Depending on the food and serving size, the actual protein content listed may be 1-2 grams more or less.

Does your child need to eat a certain amount of protein at each meal? Do you need to space protein intake evenly throughout the day? Answer: no. It would be nice if each meal had the same amount of protein, but in reality that's not practical and not necessary. The reality of eating is that food intake and food choices vary from day to day and week to week. And protein digestion and absorption will vary as well.

As long as your teen's *average* protein intake is adequate, he or she will be fine. What you don't want is for the average intake to be consistently below the minimum recommendations. That can happen when no one is paying attention, and most of the diet is junky snack foods, soft drinks and sweets.

NUTRITION AND THE MEATLESS TEEN

Protein is important, but it's not the only nutrient of concern for vegetarian teens. Teenagers are still growing, and several other key nutrients may be lacking if a vegetarian diet is poorly planned. While becoming vegetarian may *sound* healthy, many teens go into this decision with no information, or poor information, about the health consequences. They think it's just a matter of switching to soy burgers. They continue to snack on junk food, super-size their soft drinks and avoid vegetables and fruit.

The key for success is information and planning. Parents still need to keep their food radar on, so to speak. And that's even more critical for vegans. Here are some key nutrients and food sources to consider for vegetarian and vegan teens:

Calcium:

Bone growth depends on calcium, and adolescence is a critical time for bone growth. Milk from cows (or goats or other animals) is high calcium. If your vegetarian is still drinking milk or eating yogurt or cheese, adequate calcium intake can be maintained. But beware alternative plant-based "milks". Just because it's white doesn't mean it's nutritionally equivalent. Except for soy, plant-based milks are naturally very low calcium. Some may be fortified with calcium (frequently the less well-absorbed calcium carbonate form), so check the label. Most soy milks are fortified and can provide an amount of calcium similar to cow's milk, but again, it's from fortification, not natural calcium.

Vitamin B12:

B12, or cobalamin, is critical for red blood cell production and numerous neurological and metabolic functions. It's *only* found in animal-sourced foods. Fortunately, vegetarians can get plenty from cow's milk, cheese, eggs and yogurt. Vegans will have a much harder time getting B12 from foods. Some soy-based meats or milks contain added B12. Meal or energy bars may also have it added. Be sure to check labels. For vegans, fortified foods will be the only way to consume this critical vitamin.

Iron

Iron is critically important for red blood cell production and numerous other metabolic systems. Young women are more prone to iron-deficiency, due to blood loss from menstruation, so adequate iron intake during the teen years is especially important. Meat is an excellent source of well-absorbed iron. While eggs have some iron, dairy foods have none, so both vegetarians and vegans need to pay attention to other sources of this key mineral. Vegetables, whole grains and legumes contain iron to varying degrees, but the form or iron in plants is less well absorbed. The best plan is to include plenty of high iron plant foods daily. Iron-fortified foods, like cereal or bread, can also contribute to intake. Some plant sources of iron are:

- Legumes (black beans, kidney beans, lentils, peas, etc.)
- Fortified cereals
- Sesame seeds and tahini
- Sunflower seeds
- Whole grains
- Nuts
- Oatmeal
- Spinach and greens like kale and chard
- Asparagus
- Potatoes
- Wheat germ
- Soy products, including tofu
- Tomatoes
- Sweet potatoes

Healthy Fats

Fat should be part of any teens diet. Healthy fats come primarily from vegetable oils used in food preparation, nuts, avocado, eggs, cheese and other dairy foods. The new US Dietary Guidelines proposal avoids limits on fats, and encourages intake of these healthy fats. Fat in food enhances flavor and satiety. It's an important source of calories for growing and active teens.

Omega-3 fats

Omega-3s are a very specific type of fat, important for immune system, brain and nerve function. There are two distinct food forms: the 18-carbon alpha linolenic acid found in nuts, seeds and vegetable oils, and the biologically active 20 and 22-carbon EPA and DHA found only in animal-sourced foods like salmon, herring and tuna. There is some metabolic conversion of the 18-carbon omega-3 in the body, but this varies considerably from one person to the next, and is not predictable.

Vegetarians and vegans have some alternative sources, such as foods fortified with algae-sourced DHA. Chickens fed fortified feed produce higher omega-3 eggs. But the amounts in these foods vary greatly. While a product label may tout "contains omega-3!", there is currently no recommended daily intake. Food companies can add tiny token amounts of these fats and still brag about them on the label.

One problem with added omega-3s: these fats are very fragile and highly susceptible to oxidation and rancidity. So food companies have extra reason not to add too much to a food product, if there's a risk the omega-3 will oxidize and affect the flavor.

The good news is that vegetarian and vegan diets can be extremely healthy. All other nutrients, from B vitamins to minerals like magnesium and potassium to anti-oxidants, healthy fats, fiber and complex carbohydrates are plentiful in plant foods. The nutritional limitations of a vegetarian or vegan diet are few compared to limitations caused by eating a meat-heavy diet, with few plant-sourced foods.

What would a healthy balanced vegetarian diet for a teen look like?

- 3 or more servings of dairy foods daily
- a variety of high protein foods at all meals each day, such as dairy, eggs, nuts, legumes and soy
- fruit and/or vegetables at all meals
- healthy fats, from plant sources, used for cooking, or in foods like nuts, avocado and eggs.
- healthy grain-based foods, such as cereals, breads, pasta, cooked grains and bakery items throughout the day
- a minimum of sugary soft drinks
- a minimum of foods with added sugar: desserts, snacks and the like
- a minimum of salty snack foods like chips
- enough protein and calories to support healthy growth and sports activities

What would an *unhealthy* vegetarian diet look like?

- Heavy use of soft drinks, coffee or tea drinks and other sweetened beverages
- Reliance on snack bars or meal bars instead of real food
- Daily consumption of soy burgers, cheese pizza and other highly processed food
- Over consumption of snack foods
- Excess calories OR highly restrictive eating and too few calories
- High intake of added sugar foods
- Avoidance of vegetables, fruit, legumes, whole grains
- Poor intake of nutrients for growth like calcium and iron
- Reliance on low-nutrient plant-based "milks"

Unfortunately, this style of eating is not uncommon. Meatless or not, plenty of teens seem to survive on nothing but manufactured convenience foods and soft drinks. Result: high intake of fat, added sugars and salt; low intake of most nutrients and fiber. It's not a recipe for good health.

Nutrition and calorie trackers

You or your teen may want to track food intake for awhile, especially when starting out on a meatless diet, to check intake of specific nutrients, such as protein. There are a number of popular calorie tracking apps. Keep in mind, popularity doesn't necessarily guarantee accuracy.

All web-based calorie trackers use the USDA food database of food values, which includes most basic foods, like fruit, vegetables, fresh meats and grain foods. Most trackers give users the ability to add nutrition information about other food products or recipes.

Unfortunately, when users enter data, mistakes can happen. Values are entered incorrectly, or in the wrong place, or not at all. Major macronutrients like protein, fat and carbohydrate are likely to be included. Certain vitamins and some minerals are more likely to have missing values. So for example, if you're monitoring B12 or vitamin D, you might get artificially low values for your teen's diet, because those numbers are missing from food values.

Some of the more widely used calorie trackers are:

My Fitness Pal (MyFitnessPal.com)
Spark People (SparkPeople.com)
My Net Diary (MyNetDiary.com)
LoseIt (LoseIt.com)
USDA Super Tracker (https://supertracker.usda.gov)

Most of the trackers have a free version, which you can try out before paying for an upgraded version with more features. Layout, design and ease of use are important features, as well as ability to add your own foods and recipes.

LESS MEAT, BETTER ENVIRONMENT

As the human population explodes, heading towards 9 billion by 2050, demand for animal foods will increase, just as our ability to produce them becomes more limited. Meat has always been a part of the human diet. But it's not just about nutrition. Meat is also a status symbol, dating back to prehistoric times and across cultures. As incomes increase in developing countries, people buy more meat. Some anthropologists who study food and culture link the status of meat to hunting prowess and masculine characteristics. Behavioral research suggests that even today, meat eaters are viewed as more masculine than vegetarians or vegans.

When people earn more money and enter the middle class, one of the first changes they make in their lifestyle is eating more meat. Food consumption data show that the global demand for meat is increasing, driven by economic growth in China and India. In the United States, meat consumption is at an historic high: an average 195 lbs. of trimmed boneless edible meat per person per year. This is 57 lbs. more than the average consumption in the 1950's. The most dramatic increase is for poultry, which more than tripled. We're drinking less milk, but eating a lot more cheese compared to the 1950's, again almost 3 times the amount.

It's a perfect storm scenario for the global food supply: exploding population collides with the energy and water demands of livestock agriculture, and the desire of all those people for more meat. *"Feed the World"*, a 2014 series in National Geographic Magazine, summarizes the challenges, presenting a balanced view. We can grow enough food for 9 billion people using the best ideas from biotechnology, organic farming and technological advances. But even with these improvements, it will not be possible for 9 billion people to gorge on an endless supply of meat. Step Four of the 5 Step plan outlined in this series is "Shift Diets" -- away from meat. The global agricultural system can only feed everyone if meat consumption is reduced.

Energy intensive agriculture

According to the United Nations Food and Agriculture Organization (FAO) 2011 report *"Energy Smart Food for People and Climate"*, 30% of the world's energy use goes towards food production, generating 20% of greenhouse gases. By 2050, the world will need 70% more food to keep up with population growth. The current rate of energy input into the food system will be unsustainable. The report advocates a switch to energy smart agriculture, with decreasing fossil fuel input, improved yields and less waste.

One of the most effective ways to meet those goals is to reduce production and consumption of animal-source foods. Compared to plant foods, livestock agriculture is extremely energy intensive.

Animals are fed grain and soybeans, which require large inputs of water and energy to grow. Fossil energy input for meat, dairy and egg production includes the energy used for cultivation, fertilizer, pesticides, harvesting, processing and transporting the feed grains, along with the energy input for raising, feeding, transporting and processing the livestock. According to National Geographic Magazine *"The End of Cheap Oil,"* raising just one steer uses more than 280 gallons of oil. Another way to look at the issue is how much energy is required to make one gram of edible protein. Rough estimates show it takes about:

9 calories of fossil-based energy to create 1 gram of plant protein
100 calories of fossil-based energy to create 1 gram of animal protein

In other words, animal protein production uses more than 10 times as much energy as plant protein production.

Remember, the average adult needs at least 56 grams of protein per day. The average USA-style meat based diet provides twice that: 112 grams of total protein; 77 of those grams come from animal products. Noted agricultural economist David Pimentel, notes that, even if animal protein intake were reduced by half, everyone would still have almost 75 grams of protein per day.

Part of the reason animal protein requires so much fossil energy input is that we feed so much of our grain crop to livestock. In "Food, Energy and Society", Pimentel and his wife Marcia write that we feed around 45 million tons of plant protein to livestock animals every year, but get only 7.5 million tons of animal protein back in return. Considering that grain production requires energy input, that's a hefty negative return on the energy resources used to grow grains.

Energy use creates a carbon footprint, so the carbon impact of food production that uses more energy will be larger. Researchers in Spain compared the carbon footprint of meals from the typical Spanish diet to meals in the average U.S. diet. The Spanish diet equaled 5.08 CO2 equivalents per day; the U.S. diet averaged 8.6 CO2 equivalents/day. Why the difference? The Mediterranean style diet in Spain relies much less on meat and more on plant foods.

The seafood industry faces growing concerns about energy use, unsustainable fishing policies, depleted fish populations and questions about the environmental impact of large scale fish farms. Fuel for long distance factory fishing ships to operate, plus the energy needed to freeze and transport fish back to port, and then distribute it across thousands of miles by plane or truck are all considerations. Coastal fishing and fish farming would require less fuel input for transportation compared to deep sea fishing.

Fish farming is an increasingly important part of the food supply chain. Fish has plenty of nutritional benefits:
- High protein
- High quality protein
- Low fat and low calorie
- Faster maturity than some land animals
- A source of important omega-3 fatty acids

But there are downsides to current fish farming techniques. Farmed fish are fed grain and other animal-based products, so total energy requirements are similar to other livestock industries. Then there's the problems caused by raising fish in ocean-based pens:

- pollution from the fish farms drifts into the open water
- farmed fish may escape and affect local wild fish populations
- diseases from farmed fish can spread to wild fish
- farmed fish may not have the same nutritional qualities as wild fish

While fish farming techniques can contribute to problems, that doesn't mean people can't solve those problems. One example is Quixotic Farming, which raises tilapia far away from oceans and rivers. The closed system facility filters waste water and creates fertilizers for farming as a by product, while producing clean-tasting fish. Some fish farms that do operate in coastal waters are using techniques that enhance sustainability while reducing the chances for pollution and diseases. Eventually fish farms may become an indispensable source of high quality sustainable protein.

Water Intensive Agriculture

Water input for livestock production is another critical environmental concern. If we were just talking about the water animals to drink, it would be a minor concern. But those animals are fed crops like soybeans and corn, which require massive amounts of water input, from irrigation or rainfall. According to The Nature Conservancy, Americans use almost 33,000 eight oz. glasses of water/day, most of it hidden. Among the top uses for "hidden" water: grazing livestock and growing grains to feed livestock. The result is that on average, animal-source protein requires almost 100 times as much water to produce as the equivalent amount of grain protein. And this estimate doesn't even include water required for processing the meat and packaging it for sale.

Beef and sheep (lamb) are the most water-intensive meats to produce. Chicken is less water intensive, but bison may be the most water-efficient meat. Bison eat little, if any, feed grain. They graze mostly on rangeland, eating native grasses rather than irrigated forage. And they are naturally adapted to require much less drinking water than cattle.

A research team from Finland recently conducted a study to assess the impact of different diets on water resources. They found that reducing animal-based foods in the diet would cut use of rainwater by 21% and use of irrigation water by 14%. Reductions varied by region. For example, Europe and Latin America would see reductions in rainwater use, while North America and the Middle East would see more reductions in irrigation water usage.

The *Water Footprint Network*'s calculator can be used to illustrate how much additional hidden water a person consumes on a high meat diet. A hypothetical person in the US consuming a high meat and dairy diet of about 1-1/2 lbs. per day total, would use over 1200 cubic meters of water per year just for food production, of which almost 950 is for meat and dairy foods. Cut back to modest meat and dairy consumption (about 2/3 lb. of both together daily) and water use is cut in half, to 600 cubic meters per year for food production, 300 of that for meat and dairy production. Take that one step further, and go vegan. Water use for all food falls to around 350 cubic meters per year, none for livestock agriculture. Clearly cutting back on meat and dairy consumption can make a huge difference in our water footprint.

Another argument for eating less meat:

The energy and water demands of livestock agriculture are bad enough. Even without those worries, consumers are starting to rebel against the idea of large factory farms, and over-crowded inhumane living conditions for animals. The use of antibiotics and growth hormones in large-scale meat, egg and dairy production is another drawback. We don't want food that's been pumped up artificially with chemicals.

Fifty years on, the push for natural, organic foods that began in the 1960's, is getting widespread cultural traction. It's not a fringe idea anymore. The exploding interest in foods that are locally grown or produced with minimal processing translates easily into an interest in local and organic meat and dairy products and sustainable agricultural practices. Throw in the energy and water use concerns, and the argument for eating less meat becomes extremely compelling.

Quality vs. Quantity when buying meat

As you transition to meals that blend plant and animal protein foods, you may find that the meat-eaters in the family end up eating less meat by default. There's a potential benefit to this: when you do buy meat, you can buy quality, rather than quantity.

Organic meat is produced without using growth stimulants or antibiotics. It may also be local, grass fed, or raised with humane practices. These qualities come at a higher price, making those meat products more expensive. But if you're cutting back on meat purchases for the family, you may find that you can afford to buy higher quality meats in small quantities.

Of course, you might see eating less meat as a way to save money, not a reason to redirect your money to more expensive meat. I completely understand that. With the rising cost of meat, it's a very valid point. It's my personal belief that supporting small, high-quality livestock producers is a good idea. Many are local businesses, so you'd be supporting the local economy. It also sends a message to large corporate meat producers that there is a market for meat that's free of chemicals, and not fattened on expensive grains or feed made with re-purposed slaughterhouse waste.

SHOPPING AND COOKING TIPS

Before you start shopping and cooking, let's be clear about your role as the parent of a vegetarian or vegan teen:

PARENTS RESPONSIBILITY:

FEED YOUR KIDS HEALTHY FOOD

NOT PARENTS RESPONSIBILITY:

BE A GOURMET COOK

You don't have to be a gourmet cook to feed your children healthy food. In fact, being a gourmet cook may get in the way of feeding your kids simple healthy food. Teens aren't typically fans of complicated food or sophisticated flavors.

Meatless or not, parents are bombarded with advice on how to feed children nutritious food. All the rules make it sound like an overwhelming complicated chore. You have to:

- cook from scratch *always*
- buy only organic food
- make sure everything is balanced
- cleverly disguise vegetables
- banish sugar,
- control calories
- serve only food your kids will absolutely love
- preside over a peaceful and harmonious dinner table.

I've raised two children and I can safely say **this is nonsense**. Feeding children is mostly chaos. When they're teenagers, it's Chaos Squared. Throwing a vegan or vegetarian into the mix just makes the chaos worse.

You may only use a recipe from this book once a month. That's something! When teens are involved, if you can have a family meal three times a week you're doing really well.

Feel free to use short cuts whenever possible. You can even resort to take-out for the basis of some of these meals. Order a cheese pizza and add your own vegetables. Buy pre-chopped vegetables. There are plenty of short cut options that don't sacrifice quality, taste or nutrition.

The process starts at the grocery store. The good news is that many of the staple foods used for vegetarian or vegan meals have a longer shelf life than fresh meat, and are easier to handle. No more dirty cutting boards or yucky meat trimmings in the trash.

Grains, nuts and beans are the key staples for meatless cooking. Stock up so you always have options for meal preparation.

1. **Nuts** come in several readily available varieties. Buy unsalted nuts from bulk bins or in cans or packages. Store them in the refrigerator in jars or plastic bags. You can buy raw or roasted nuts. Roasting or toasting for a few minutes in a moderate oven can improve the flavor.
2. **Beans** (or legumes or pulses) are plant protein stars. You can buy dried beans and cook them yourself, but I highly recommend just buying canned beans. They're so much easier, and are ready to use for last minute meal preparation. Buy unsalted when available. For some recipes, you need to drain liquid from the can of beans. For salads made with canned beans, it helps to rinse the canning liquid off of the beans.
3. **Whole grains** come in many varieties, but we're accustomed to just a few, such as wheat and rice. Quinoa is a new entrant in our whole grain cuisine, and many grocery stores are stocking interesting exotic grains, some pre-cooked. While grains aren't as high in protein as legumes, they do contain key amino acids, as discussed previously, that complement the amino acids in legumes or nuts. They're also delicious and filling and add variety to meals.
4. **Oils** add flavor and satiety to recipes. I recommend using olive oil or canola oil for most food preparation and salad dressings. While I prefer olive oil in small bottles with the origin of the olives clearly listed, I realize many people don't want to spend the extra money for those. The cheaper olive oils are typically made with mixtures of olives from several countries. If you buy

single-origin oil, you'll notice the taste difference. Sesame and peanut oils are also useful for meatless cooking.

5. When buying **vegetables**, fresh is best, and fresh in season is best of all. But canned and frozen vegetables can be just fine and add convenience to your shopping and cooking. Fresh vegetables have to be used up in a timely fashion or they spoil. And that's a waste of lovely food and of your money.

6. **High protein ingredients** – whether meats, cheese or soy foods -- are used as condiments, and are prepared separately, depending on the number of meat eaters, vegetarians and vegans in the family. Recommendations for protein foods that work well with each recipe are provided.

Protein Condiments

High protein foods, added as condiments, are the key to making the recipes work for everyone in the family. The meat-eaters can have meat; the vegetarians and vegans have alternative protein sources.

Options for protein condiments are listed with each recipe (except some bean recipes), in suggested per-serving amounts. You may find that some family members want more of the protein foods. If you are trying to cut back on meat consumption anyway, the meat eaters can also include the vegan or vegetarian protein foods to boost overall protein intake.

Here are some general descriptions of the different high protein foods you can choose from:

- *Red meat: Beef, pork lamb, bison:*
  One ounce of cooked red meat has roughly 7 grams of protein. Leaner meat has slightly higher protein content.
- *Chicken/Turkey:*
  One ounce of cooked white meat chicken or turkey has just over 8 grams of protein.
- *Fish*
  One ounce of cooked fish has between 6 and 8 grams of protein
- *Tofu:*
  An ounce of tofu has 2-3 grams of protein. Before sautéing

tofu, slice and let sit on paper towels to drain off some of the moisture.

- *Nuts/nut butters:*
  1/4 cup nuts weighs about 1 ounce. Protein ranges from 4-6 grams, depending on which nut you choose. A scant 2 TB nut butter has about the same nutritional content as 1 oz. of nuts.

- *Eggs*
  1 egg has 6-7 grams of protein, depending on egg size.

- *Cheese*
  Protein varies depending on the fat and moisture content of the cheese. Cheeses, like cheddar or Swiss, have about 7 grams of protein per 1 oz. Feta has 4. Hard grating cheeses, like Parmesan, have around 10 grams protein per oz. Cheese with high water content, like cottage cheese, are measured by the cup, and are very high protein.

- *Yogurt*
  Protein content varies according to fat content, moisture content and added ingredients like fruit. Greek style yogurt tends to be much higher protein because water is strained out. Protein in regular plain yogurt is similar to the protein in milk: about 8 grams per cup.

- *Milk/soy milk*
  The recipes in this book don't typically use milk as an ingredient. However, many people – especially teens -- drink milk with meals, which adds high quality protein. If someone in the family usually drinks milk with the meal, you can think of milk as the complementary protein to a vegetarian dish. This saves having to prepare an additional high protein food.

NOTE: alternative "milks" made from plants like almonds and coconut are **not high protein** and do not qualify as complementary protein foods.

Cooking sequence

If you're cooking a meal for both meat eaters and vegetarians/vegans, the cooking sequence for the protein foods can be important. If you need to sauté sliced meat as well as tofu, you could use one frying pan for each item. Never cook all of these together in one pan at the same time. But, if you only have one frying pan or you don't want to get so many pans dirty, follow this sequence.

1. Cook the vegetables first. Don't over cook. Put them in a serving dish or plate that's heat proof and hold in a warm (250) oven.
2. Add a bit of oil and cook the tofu next.
3. Meat last. Add a bit more oil and cook sliced meat at higher heat until it's browned, stirring constantly until the pieces are cooked through. Sliced meat will cook quickly.
4. Another method for meat: grill, sauté or broil the meat in whole pieces and then slice it up before eating. This works well for steak, chicken breast and chops or tenderloin.

If you follow this sequence, you avoid vegans or vegetarians objecting to meat juice soaking into the tofu or whatever else you're cooking. This is a valid concern, so either use separate pans, or cook protein foods in that order.

Tips for adding nuts to your recipes

Nuts add flavor and crunch to meatless meals, and are useful in hot dishes and salads. But after they sit in a casserole or salad overnight, they may become soft and lose their flavor. If you're going to have leftovers, the best solution is to have people add nuts to their food at the table, and store leftover nuts separately from the leftovers.

Meal planning strategies:

A one pot meal is easy for the cook, but side dishes are a good idea. They add variety of flavor, texture and nutrients. They absolutely do not need to be complicated. Bread or a simple fruit salad are good options. The recipes include suggestions for easy side dishes that complement the main dish and add variety in flavors, textures and nutrients.

Don't overlook the importance of texture. Most people don't think much about that when planning vegetarian meals. Meat is chewy; it has a unique texture that vegetables, grains, beans and dairy foods just don't have. The softer texture of cooked grains, noodles and beans can be monotonous. There are several easy solutions:

Don't overcook the vegetables.

Use protein add-ins that have texture, such as nuts for vegans or meat for the carnivores

Add side dishes with different textures: crunchy fresh raw vegetables, chewy artisanal bread, nuts, and raw fruit. Plus those foods add nutrients, so it's a win-win solution.

Adding meat to the meal

Meat as a condiment: These recipes are designed to use meat as a condiment. It can be cooked (or heated) and served separately, so the meat-eaters can help themselves. This is a good way to use up leftover cooked meat. Or you can cook small pieces of meat, such as chicken tenders or ground meat.

Meat as a side dish: Sometimes nothing will do except a steak, chicken breast, salmon filet or rack of ribs. The key word here is "sometimes". The best strategy to cut back on meat while still enjoying those foods is to eat them occasionally. Not everyday. Not every meal.

Consider this approach: two to three times a week, cook separate pieces of meat (easy things like grilled chicken, burgers, steak or chop) for the meat eaters in the family, while still serving a meatless entree. The meat eaters will be happy, and the vegetarians or vegans will still have a tasty and nutritious main dish. For the rest of the family meals, stick to meatless dishes.

Get Your Kids Involved!

If your teenager wants to be a vegetarian, then **he or she needs to be involved in the process.** And one important part of this process is identifying plant foods that he or she will eat. Grains, beans, nuts and tofu are great, but vegetarians aren't obliged to like all of them.

Have a family taste test event. Visit your local grocery or natural foods store and buy 5-6 different grains in small amounts (it helps if your store sells grains in bulk bins, so you can take just the amount you want). Quinoa, buckwheat, brown rice, basmati rice, couscous, millet and barley are good choices. Cook them according to package directions and let everyone taste a small amount. Serve the grains plain so you get the full flavor. Everyone can vote for his or her favorites, and hopefully your teen will identify at least 3 that are acceptable. You can do the same for any other unfamiliar foods, such as different beans or legumes, or types of noodles or nuts.

If you feel like the rest of the family needs to ease into this idea, **try serving the meatless entrée as a side dish** along with your usual dinner. Your vegetarian teen will have something to eat, and everyone else can do the taste test thing. That's a good plan if you're worried that a particular meatless recipe may not be a big hit.

Remember, there's no reason everyone has to dive right into a new way of eating overnight. For most families, that's *not* a good plan. Taste testing new dishes, involving your resident vegetarian in the planning, and allowing everyone to participate is a better path to success.

Notes about the recipes

- The recipes are written for someone who is comfortable with simple cooking techniques.
- You don't need any fancy equipment. A good sauté pan, sauce pan, large pot, 2-3 sharp knives, mixing bowls, measuring cups and cutting board are essential. A food processor can be very helpful, especially for chopping nuts.
- Serving sizes are for modest portions eaten by an average adult, as part of a meal with side dishes. But of course, if you're feeding teenagers, serving size could be the entire recipe. Plan accordingly. It's easy to double or even triple the recipes to accommodate your teen's appetite. Most of the recipes work fine as leftovers.
- Nutrition information per serving is given at the end of each recipe. Nutrient calculations always have some margin of error, depending on your measuring and cooking techniques, amount and type of protein condiment used and how much oil is used for the sauté pan.

BEANS

Whether you call them beans, legumes or pulses, they're all high protein.

Humans have been eating legumes for centuries. Green beans, peas, kidney beans, lentils, soy beans and even peanuts are all officially legumes. And they're true nutrition super stars, high in:

- Protein
- Potassium
- Magnesium
- Fiber
- Iron
- Calcium
- B vitamins

As noted in Chapter 3, bean protein is low in the amino acid methionine, so combining a bean dish with a higher methionine food -- such as a cooked grain, or bread or dairy food – will increase the overall quality of the protein in that meal.

These beans recipes use canned beans whenever possible, to increase convenience. In some cases, quick-cooking legumes, like lentils, are essential ingredients. Or course, you can cook your own dried beans if you like.

VEGETARIAN BEAN BURGERS

Making your own meatless burgers isn't complicated. But it is different. Ground meat holds together, and has a firm, chewy texture when cooked. Pre-packaged soy and veggie burgers are processed to have a similar texture to meat. They're easy, and for plenty of non-meat-eaters, soy burgers are a dietary mainstay. While they're not terrible, they can be loaded with seasonings, texturizers, and other additives to make them look and taste like meat. If you're avoiding meat, why eat processed fake meat?

The best ingredient for making meatless burgers at home is beans. They're high protein, come in many different flavors, have a good texture for burger-making, and work with many different seasonings.

Bean burgers are not at all difficult to make. The whole family can enjoy them. But if you have just one vegetarian family member, you can mix up a batch of bean burgers, and freeze them wrapped individually, making family burger dinners that much easier.

Preparation Notes:

- Avoiding eggs? Substitute 1 TB chia gel* for one egg.
- The burgers can be customized by using different beans or varying the seasonings and the toppings.
- You can mix up a batch, shape the burgers, wrap in plastic and freeze for use another time.
- These will not hold up to cooking on a grill grate.
- Makes 4 bean burgers.

Ingredients:

- 1 large clove of garlic, or about 1-1/2 tsp. chopped garlic, or to taste

- 1/4 cup grated Parmesan (about 1/4 cup of packaged grated Parmesan)

- 1 15-oz can of beans. Use pinto, white kidney or butter beans

- 1/4 cup plain panko crumbs plus more for coating the burgers

- 1 egg or 1 TB chia gel

- 1 tsp. dried basil (or 2 TB chopped fresh basil leaves)

- ¼ tsp. dried oregano

- Salt and pepper

- 1-2 TB olive, corn or peanut oil for the sauté pan

Make the burgers

1. Drain the beans, saving the liquid in a small bowl. You'll have about 1-1/2 cup of beans and ½ - 2/3 cup liquid.

2. Put the garlic, Parmesan, 3/4 cup of the drained beans, ¼ cup of the bean liquid, 1/4 cup of the panko, egg, seasonings, pinch of salt and pepper in food processor. Blend until smooth.

3. Add the rest of the beans. Process briefly, so you still see small chunks of the beans. The mixture should *slightly* moist, but not watery, close to the texture of ground meat. If it's too dry (doesn't hold together at all), add 1-2 TB more of the liquid from the beans.

4. Spread a layer of panko crumbs on a small plate.

5. Form 3-4 patties with the bean mixture. If it's too sticky and not holding together, add another 1-2 TB of Panko crumbs and let it sit for a few minutes.

6. As you form each patty, quickly put it on the panko crumbs on the plate. Flip over to coat both sides. Lightly press the crumbs into the burger.

7. Set the finished patties on a plate on waxed paper, parchment or plastic wrap, and refrigerate for at least 1/2 hour.

8. Fry in a pan, brushed with a bit of olive oil, or use a non-stick pan. Olive oil gives a nicer flavor.

9. When is it done? Bean burgers don't cook quite as firmly as ground meat burgers. But they will hold together when done. Depending on your pan, they may take 3-4 minutes per side. The burgers should be browned on both sides.

10. Serve on toasted burger buns, with your choice of sliced tomatoes, sliced avocado, lettuce, arugula, sliced onion, sautéed peppers and/or mushrooms, ketchup, BBQ sauce, mustard or other condiments of your choice.

11. Boost the protein with thin sliced cheese, such as mozzarella, cheddar, Swiss, Jack or Muenster. Cheese adds about 7 grams of protein per ounce.

Side dishes:
- baked sweet potatoes or baked potatoes
- sautéed greens (spinach, kale, chard, beet greens) and mushrooms
- tossed green salad

Leftovers? You can reheat cooked bean burgers in the microwave briefly.

190 calories • 9 gr protein • 9 gr fat • 19 g carbs • 5 gr fiber
Fat and calories will vary according to how much oil is used for cooking

*Make Chia Gel

Chia seed has been a staple food in Central and South America for centuries. It's a source of fiber, calcium and omega-3 fats. When mixed with water, it forms a gel, which can be used as an egg substitute in some dishes, or mixed into beverages or cooked food. Make the gel:

- Mix 2 TB chia seeds with 1 cup water.

- Let stand for 15 minutes, stirring with a fork every 2-3 minutes to prevent clumping.

- Substitute 1 TB of gel for one egg in bean burger recipes.

- You can save the unused gel in a sealed jar in the refrigerator to use within a few days.

VEGAN BLACK BEAN BURGERS

Making vegan burgers is a bit tricky, but not impossible. Meat burgers are easy, because the meat holds its shape. Meatless burgers made with egg hold together better once they're cooked, thanks to the egg. So the main problem with egg-less and meat-less burgers is that they don't hold together as well.

This means you have to be more careful handling the uncooked burgers. It also means you have the opportunity to investigate ingredients. This recipe uses chia gel, but there are many other vegan burger recipes out there that use oats or cooked grains or different vegetables.

Vegan burgers will be lower protein than burgers with meat or egg. You can boost the meal's protein content with soy milk, or add other protein ingredients like nuts to side dishes.

Ingredients for 4 burgers:
- 1 15 oz. can black beans
- 1 heaping TB chia gel*
- 1/4 tsp. cumin
- ½ tsp. ground coriander
- optional: 1/8 tsp. cayenne pepper OR 1 TB minced jalapeño (to taste, depending on how hot your jalapenos are)
- 1 tsp. mild chile powder
- 1-2 tsp. minced fresh garlic
- ¼ cup crushed corn tortilla chips
- ¼ cup finely chopped unsalted toasted almonds
- 1/4 cup Panko crumbs, plus more on a plate for coating
- ¼ tsp. salt
- 1-2 TB corn, peanut or olive oil for cooking

250 calories • 8 gr protein • 7 gr fat • 28 g carbs • 7 gr fiber
Fat and calories will vary according to how much oil is used for cooking

Make the burgers

1. Drain the beans, saving the liquid in a small bowl. You'll have about 1-1/2 cup of beans and 2/3 cup liquid.

2. Put the garlic, crushed chips, 3/4 cup of the drained beans, ¼ cup of the bean liquid, 1/4 cup of the panko, chia gel and seasonings in food processor. Blend until smooth.

3. Add the rest of the beans. Process briefly, so you still see small chunks of the beans. The mixture should *slightly* moist, but not watery, close to the texture of ground meat. If it's too dry (doesn't hold together at all), add 1-2 TB more of the liquid from the beans.

4. Mix the Panko crumbs and pulverized almonds in a bowl. Spread a layer of crumbs on a small plate.

5. Form 4 patties with the bean mixture. If the mixture is too sticky and not holding together, add another 1-2 TB of Panko crumbs and let it sit for a few minutes.

6. As you form each patty, quickly put it on the crumbs on the plate. Flip over to coat both sides with crumbs. Lightly press the crumbs into the burger.

7. Set the finished patties on a plate on waxed paper, parchment or plastic wrap, and refrigerate for at least 1/2 hour.

8. Heat the oil in a sauté pan. Cook until burgers are browned on one side. Flip over and brown the other side. Each side may take 3-4 minutes, depending on your pan.

9. When are they done? Burgers should hold their shape, although without eggs, vegan burgers will be softer on the inside, not chewy like cooked meat.

Serve on toasted burger buns. Suggested toppings: sliced tomato, lettuce leaves, sliced avocado or guacamole, sliced red onion, slices of roasted chile or roasted red pepper, chopped fresh sweet peppers, salsa.

If you want a more gourmet burger, top with a good quality molé sauce or Thai peanut curry sauce.

Side dishes:
- Sautéed sweet potato slices
- Corn on the cob
- Warmed tortillas
- Chopped salad with tomatoes and cucumbers
- Tossed green salad with toasted almonds

Best bean choices

make burgers: black, pinto, kidney, garbanzo

add to soups: kidney, garbanzo, navy lentils, black eyed peas

add to salads: garbanzo, kidney, black, edamame

for cooked bean dishes: kidney, pinto, black, lentils, black eyed peas

Stock your pantry with a variety of canned beans so you're always ready to boost protein in a variety of recipes by adding beans.

Black eyed peas and edamame are available frozen.

BLACK BEAN SALAD

Bean salads are some of the easiest dishes to prepare, and are great for quick summer meals. Serve bean salads with a complementary grain dish, or just some wonderful crusty bread.

Thanks to the beans and vegetables, this refreshing salad is very filling.

HINT: keep some cans of beans in the frig, ready to go when you decide to whip up a bean salad at the last minute. That way your finished salad will be cold.

Ingredients (serves 2 people generously)
- one 15 oz. can of black beans, drained and rinsed briefly.
- 1 cup corn kernels (or corn cut from a cooked ear of fresh corn)
- 1 TB minced jalapeno (to taste)
- ½ avocado, cut into chunks
- 2 fresh tomatoes, cut into bite-sized pieces
- 2-3 chopped scallions
- juice from one lime
- ¼ cup chopped fresh cilantro
- salt and pepper to taste

Protein condiment options per serving:
- Vegans: 1 oz. crumbled soft tofu
  340 calories • 20 gr protein • 9 gr fat • 56 g carbs • 18 gr fiber
- Vegetarians: 1 oz. crumbled feta or goat cheese
  400 calories • 23 gr protein • 14 gr fat • 57 g carbs • 18 gr fiber
- Meat eaters: this recipe works just fine without any meat. If you must, use 1-2 oz. cooked shrimp per serving
  360 calories • 25 gr protein • 8 gr fat • 56 g carbs • 18 gr fiber

Make the salad

1. Mix all the ingredients together, season with salt and pepper to taste. Adjust jalapeno and lime juice to suit your taste.
2. If you make this ahead of time, refrigerate before serving.

Side dishes:
- cooked grain salad (see Grains chapter for ideas)
- cornbread or French bread
- fresh berries or sliced fresh melon.

Other bean salad ingredient variations:

1. Garbanzo beans, chopped tomatoes, sweet peppers, red onion, chopped seeded cucumbers, basil, oregano, mint, lemon juice. Optional fresh mozzarella cheese.

2. Kidney beans, chopped tomatoes, cooked corn, chopped scallions, chopped celery, minced fresh basil, lemon or lime juice, Optional: diced fresh mozzarella or goat cheese

MINESTRONE

A hearty bean soup might be the winter-time equivalent of bean salads – really easy to throw together. Soup is not complicated and doesn't have to simmer for hours to taste good. Added bonus: it's very filling. Minestrone is loaded with vegetables, making it extra nutritious.

Ingredients (plenty for 4 people. This soup is thick and hearty. If you like a thinner soup, use more broth.

- 2 cups packaged or home-made vegetarian broth**
- 1 can beans, not drained: kidney, white kidney, navy
- 1 15-oz can diced or crushed tomatoes
- 2 TB olive oil
- ½ cup onion, chopped
- ½ cup chopped celery
- ½ chopped carrot
- 1 TB minced garlic
- 1 tsp. dried oregano
- ¼ tsp. dried thyme
- 1 cup frozen chopped spinach
- 1/2 cup frozen green beans

Protein condiment options per serving:

o   Vegans: 2 oz. meatless sausage
330 calories • 17 gr protein • 10 gr fat • 47 g carbs • 13 gr fiber

o   Vegetarians: ¼ cup grated Parmesan or other hard grating cheese OR ¼ cup grated mozzarella
330 calories • 19 gr protein • 15 gr fat • 35 g carbs • 11 gr fiber

o   Meat eaters: 2 oz. cooked chicken or turkey OR 2 oz. low fat Italian sausage
300 calories • 27 gr protein • 9 gr fat • 34 g carbs • 11 gr fiber

Make the soup

1. Sauté the onion, celery and carrot until soft, with the herbs and garlic.
2. Put everything in a large pot and bring to a boil.
3. Turn the heat down right away and simmer for about 5 minutes to make sure the frozen vegetables are heated through.
4. Add protein condiments when serving.

Side dishes:
- Bread: pita, French or cornbread work nicely
- Bruschetta
- open-faced toasted cheese or nut butter sandwiches
- Tossed salad (you can add cooked meat, cheese or nuts)

Bean soup ingredient variations:
1. Black beans, tomatoes, onion, chile peppers, garlic, cumin, cilantro.
2. Garbanzo beans, tomatoes, spinach/chard, zucchini, garlic, basil.

Fancier Serving Idea

Serve the soup in cooked winter squash boats.

- Use Acorn or similar winter squash

- Cut in half lengthwise and scoop out the seeds.

- Put face down on a greased baking sheet and cook until the shells are barely fork-tender, not falling apart.

- Turn over onto shallow serving bowl and fill with bean soup. Garnish with protein condiments and sprinkle with chopped parsley.

The winter squash adds plenty of nutrients, plus it's filling, always a benefit when you're feeding teenagers.

*Make vegetarian broth:

It's easy to make your own vegetarian soup broth. Fill a large pot 2/3 up with chopped vegetables: onions, celery, carrots, mushrooms, greens, cabbage and other vegetables that work well cooked. Mushrooms make an especially flavorful broth.

Don't overwhelm your vegetable mix with too much broccoli, cauliflower or hot peppers. It's best to use mostly vegetables that you typically cook, rather than salad vegetables like lettuce.

Add enough water to cover the vegetables with an inch of water.

Bring to a boil, and turn the heat down to simmer the vegetables for an hour or more, adding water as necessary.

Drain the liquid into a bowl and cool. Discard the vegetables.

Put the cooled broth into storage containers that suit your needs. Freeze unused broth.

CHILI

Chili is very easily adapted to the meat-eating preferences of different family members. If you're cooking meat for some people, just cook it separately. Bean chili is delicious and high protein without any meat. Vegetarians can boost the protein by topping with grated cheese.

The ingredients for chili are very simple; it's the seasonings that make it unique and uniquely yours. There are plenty of suggestions here, and you can increase or decrease them to your taste.

Ingredients
- 2 15-oz cans beans. Use two different types if you like. Choose from pinto, kidney and black beans.
- 1 onion, chopped
- 2-3 TB corn, olive or other oil for sautéing
- 1 15-oz can crushed or diced tomatoes
- 1 TB minced garlic
- 1-2 small (6 oz.) cans roasted chiles
- 1 TB paprika OR 1 TB ground chile powder (not chili seasoning mix) or a combination of these. The amount of chile should be adjusted to your taste preferences and chile heat. Ground ancho or chipotle are hotter and add rich flavor.
- 2 tsp. oregano
- 1 tsp. cumin
- 1 tsp. ground coriander
- ½ tsp. salt, or to taste (depends on whether canned beans were salted)
- OPTIONAL: ½ minced jalapeno or other fresh hot chile
- OPTIONAL: ¼ to ½ cup finely chopped fresh cilantro

Protein condiment options per serving:

o Vegans: the beans are high protein, but you can add 2 oz. crumbled meat alternatives to enhance the flavor.
   420 calories • 24 gr protein • 14 gr fat • 44 g carbs • 16 gr fiber

o Vegetarians: ¼ cup grated cheddar or Jack cheese OR 2-3 TB Greek style yogurt (use like sour cream)
   Cheese: 430 calories • 19 gr protein • 21 gr fat • 44 g carbs • 13 gr fiber
   Yogurt: 340 calories • 17 gr protein • 12 gr fat • 47 g carbs • 13 gr fiber

o Meat eaters: 2 oz. cooked ground beef, turkey or bison
   440 calories • 27 gr protein • 18 gr fat • 44 g carbs • 13 gr fiber

Make the chili

1. Sauté the onion in oil with the garlic, until onion is soft.
2. Drain off about half the liquid from each can of beans and add to the pot.
3. Add the tomatoes, chiles and spices.
4. Cook meat separately, if using.
5. Grate cheese, ¼ to ½ cup per serving. Jack, Colby and Cheddar are good choices.

Side dishes:
- Warmed tortillas
- Cornbread
- Tossed green salad
- Chunky tomato, corn and avocado salad
- Guacamole and raw veggie sticks
- Fruit salad

CASSOULET

Cassoulet is like European chili. It's based on beans, but the flavorings are more European than Mexican. And as with chili, there are endless ways to make it. Traditionally cassoulet contains bacon, duck and sausages. This recipe is a modified version, much simpler to make.

Because the flavor of cassoulet depends on the meaty flavor of sausages, the suggested vegan protein is meatless sausage. The meat eaters in your family can add real bacon and/or sausage to their own servings. Those are easy to prepare separately.

You can serve this dish right away, but the flavors will improve if it simmers for awhile. If you make it ahead, put the cassoulet in a heavy-duty casserole with a lid, and keep in a 300° oven for an hour before serving. Check every 15-20 minutes, and add a bit of water or tomato juice if it's drying out.

Ingredients for 4 generous servings

- 2 cans white kidney beans (navy beans are OK too)
- 2 TB olive oil for the sauté pan
- 1 onion, chopped
- 1 stalk celery, chopped
- 1 carrot, chopped
- 1 15 oz. can diced tomatoes, with juice
- 2 cloves garlic, minced
- 1 bay leaf
- ¼ tsp. dried thyme
- ¼ tsp. red pepper flakes, or to taste
- grated rind of ½ lemon
- 1 TB Dijon mustard
- ½ tsp. salt, or to taste
- ¼ tsp. black pepper
- OPTIONAL: 1 TB chopped fresh parsley

Protein condiment options per serving:

o Vegans: 1-2 oz. crumbled meat alternative, such as a soy burger OR 1-2 oz. meatless sausage.
  380 calories • 22 gr protein • 12 gr fat • 43 g carbs • 13 gr fiber

o Vegetarians: ¼ cup grated Parmesan, Romano or other hard cheese OR ¼ cup grated mozzarella
  360 calories • 20 gr protein • 11 gr fat • 39 g carbs • 12 gr fiber

o Meat eaters: 1-2 oz. cooked sausage or diced ham. 1 slice crumbled bacon adds flavor although little protein.
  340 calories • 18 gr protein • 8 gr fat • 39 g carbs • 12 gr fiber

Make the cassoulet

1. Heat 2 TB olive oil in a large pot and sauté the onions, celery, carrots and garlic with the thyme.
2. Add the beans (with the liquid from the can), tomatoes, bay leaf, parsley, cheese rind and pepper flakes.
3. Heat through and simmer for ½ hour, adding vegetable broth as necessary.
4. Cook optional bacon and sausage; chop ham.
5. Remove the cheese rind before serving.

Side dishes:

▪ Crusty French-style bread, preferably whole grain, or bruschetta.
▪ Tossed green salad with additional protein foods such as walnuts and grated cheese.
▪ Roasted Brussels sprouts or a mix of Brussels sprouts, broccoli and cauliflower

DAL (CURRIED LENTIL SOUP)

While the word "dal" cam refer to all Indian dishes made with legumes. many Indian cookbooks and restaurants use the term to refer to thick curried soups made with lentils.

You may be familiar with the brown-colored lentils available in grocery stores, but in fact there are many varieties of lentils, from pink to black to green. If your grocery store doesn't carry the more exotic varieties, try natural food groceries or ethnic food shops.

Cooking time for dried lentils is much shorter than for regular dried beans, such as kidney beans. But they do require more time than canned beans, so plan ahead if you'll be serving dal. You can cook the lentils ahead of time if necessary.

Dal is best served with other Indian style foods. It goes great with a rice dish, or the traditional flatbread naan (or warmed pita breads), plain yogurt and a spicy vegetable dish. If you like Indian curries, experiment with other dal recipes that are spiced differently and use different types of lentils.

This recipe is very basic and one of my favorites, using the lentils you can easily find in the grocery store. This is more like a soup.

Ingredients for 3 hearty servings:

- 1 cup lentils, rinsed
- 3 cups water
- 2 TB peanut or other bland oil
- 1 TB fresh jalapeno, minced (or use an amount to taste)
- 1 tsp. ground ginger
- 1 10-oz package frozen chopped spinach
- juice of one lemon (about 2 TB)
- ½ tsp. turmeric
- 1 tsp. ground coriander
- ½ tsp. ground cumin
- ¼ cup chopped fresh cilantro
- ½ tsp. salt, or to taste

Protein condiment options per serving:

- Vegans: 2 oz. plain soy yogurt as garnish
  380 calories • 22 gr protein • 11 gr fat • 51 g carbs • 23 gr fiber
- Vegetarians: ¼ cup plain Greek style yogurt as garnish
  370 calories • 26 gr protein • 11 gr fat • 45 g carbs • 22 gr fiber
- Meat eaters: 2 oz. cooked chicken
  420 calories • 38 gr protein • 12 gr fat • 43 g carbs • 22 gr fiber

Make the Dal

1. Bring the water to a boil and add the lentils
2. Reduce heat and simmer until the lentils are soft, 35-40 minutes.
3. Towards the end of the cooking time, put the chopped frozen spinach in the pot, so it thaws and cooks with the lentils.
4. Add the oil, lemon juice and spices to the pot and heat through.
5. Add the chopped cilantro last, before serving.

Side dishes:
- Raita, a condiment made with plain yogurt, herbs and vegetables or fruit
- Flat bread like naan, pita or warmed tortillas
- Rice, plain or a curried dish
- A curry-spiced vegetable dish (if the dish includes ground nuts, that will boost the protein content)

Indian cuisine gives us a great example of how to think about plant protein foods. Unlike the Western tradition of serving the protein as a large portion of meat, Indian foods spread the protein out among 2-4 dishes.

A meal might include a legume dish, a grain-based food (rice, naan), a yogurt raita and a vegetable dish, with nuts or seeds used in one of more of these dishes. Result: a variety of complementary plant protein foods included in the meal, but not all in the same dish.

This way of composing meals creates more variety of flavors and textures. Plus it covers a lot of nutritional bases. Most of the recipes include vegetables, which contribute to nutritional balance.

But you don't need to serve Indian food to create this type of food mix. Meatless dishes in all types of flavors – from Mexican to Asian to European and on – are amenable to this type of meal planning.

SAUTÉED GARBANZO BEANS

Make this really easy dish ahead for quick snacks, or use as a side dish for a grain or pasta-based meal.

Ingredients for 4 modest servings:
- One 15 oz. can garbanzo beans
- Peanut, corn or other flavorless oil
- spice mix of your choice, such as:
  - o 1 tsp. garam masala
  - o 2 tsp. minced garlic + ½ tsp. cumin + pinch of cayenne
  - o 1 tsp. curry powder
  - o 1 tsp. ground chile powder
- salt to taste
- optional: plain yogurt as a garnish

1. Drain the can of beans in a sieve. Rinse well under the faucet and let excess water drip out.
2. Put a paper towel on a plate and spread the drained beans on it. Put another paper towel on top. Let sit for 15-20 minutes.
3. Heat 2 TB oil over moderate heat in a large skillet, big enough so that the beans will form one layer in the pan.
4. When the oil is hot, spread the dried garbanzos on the pan, and cover with a splatter screen.
5. Sauté the beans for about 10 minutes, stirring frequently to prevent scorching. Adjust heat as necessary. After about 5 minutes, sprinkle the spices over the beans and stir thoroughly to distribute the spices over the beans.
6. Continue cooking until slightly browned. Serve right away. Add salt to taste at the table.

150 calories • 6 gr protein • 8 gr fat • 16 g carbs • 6 gr fiber

Sautéed garbanzo beans can boost the protein in meatless meals and snacks. Here are a few ideas:

- Roll some in a wrap or tortilla spread with tahini, garnished with chopped cucumber.

- Mix shredded carrot, chopped cashews and sliced scallions for a quick snack salad.

- Dress with plain yogurt and serve as a side dish to a curried rice or potato dish.

- Make a pita sandwich with hummus, chopped tomato, lettuce and sautéed garbanzos.

- Add to a tossed green salad.

- Use to spice up tomato soup.

- Serve warm with a squeeze of lemon or lime juice as a high protein side dish.

Make a big batch and refrigerate for easy use.

MUKIMAME SALAD

Soybeans are legumes, just like black beans or garbanzo beans. Legumes grow in pods (think peas in pods). For most legumes, we remove the seeds from the pods. Although for sugar snap peas we eat the whole pod.

When soybeans are picked green, they're a lot like green peas. Compared to cooked dried beans, fresh soybeans have higher natural water content and are sweeter and crunchier.

Edamame refers to green soy beans still in the pods. You can buy those frozen or fresh. Cooked in the pod, they make a fun snack.

Mukimame refers to green soybeans that have been removed from the pod. You can find them frozen, and they cook quickly, much like green peas, not like dried beans.

This salad emphasizes mukimame's fresh flavor and crunchy texture. It's a great dish to complement a grain-based salad for a warm weather dinner. Because mukimame is high protein by itself, you don't need any other high protein ingredients for this dish.

Ingredients
- One 16 oz. bag frozen mukimame.
- 2 TB olive, canola or peanut oil
- 1-2 TB lemon juice, or to taste
- ½ cup sliced scallions
- 2 cups chopped fresh tomatoes
- 1 sweet red pepper, chopped
- 1 avocado, chopped
- 1-2 cloves garlic, minced
- salt and pepper to taste
- optional: ½ jalapeno minced

Make the mukimame salad:

1. Cook the mukimame according to package instructions. Many packages recommend microwaving in the bag. Don't overcook. Mushy mukimame isn't desirable for this recipe.
2. Put the cooled mukimame in a large mixing bowl.
3. Chop all the vegetables and add to the bowl.
4. Mix in the oil, garlic and lemon juice.
5. Season with salt and pepper to taste
6. Refrigerate before serving. The flavor will improve if the salad is allowed to sit for 30 or so minutes.

225 calories • 16 gr protein • 13 gr fat • 12 g carbs • 8 gr fiber

You can boost the protein even more by garnishing with fresh mozzarella or feta cheese, or for vegans, chopped toasted walnuts or pecans.

GRAINS

Humans have been eating grains for thousands of years. They remain a staple food around the world, providing calories, vitamins, minerals and protein. Grains are seeds, and many, such as wheat and rye, are seeds of Grass Family plants. Others, like buckwheat and quinoa, are seeds from other types of plants. Whatever the plant source, the seeds have to be cooked in water or ground into flour or meal.

Grains make a great base for a one-pot meal, and they combine nicely with all types of protein foods, from meat to beans to nuts. The humble peanut butter sandwich is a well-known example of combining a grain with another plant food for a more complete protein.

Here is a list of some of the grains you may find in your local grocery store:

- Barley
- Bulgur wheat
- Millet
- Rice: there are numerous varieties, from easy-to-find brown and white varieties, to Arborio, Basmati and Jasmine, to the more exotic black or red rice.
- Corn: fresh sweet corn, corn meal, posole (made with dried whole corn kernels), polenta (made with coarsely ground corn meal and used in Italian cooking)
- Quinoa
- Keff
- Farro
- Whole wheat: whole wheat flour, whole wheat berries
- Rye
- Oats: rolled oats, steel cut oats
- Amaranth
- Buckwheat
- Wild rice

That's a lot of possibilities. They all have distinctive flavors, from the subtle taste of white rice to the nutty flavor of millet to the stronger flavor of buckwheat. Some blend more or less successfully with certain vegetables, cheeses, meats, beans and nuts. Buy 3-5 different grains and hold a family taste test event to see which are liked best.

The recipes in this chapter use a specific grain, but feel free to substitute others to create your own signature family recipes.

Grain Cooking Tips

1. For simmering whole grains, the grain-to-liquid ratios and cooking times vary from one grain to another. Check cooking instructions on the package.
2. In most cases, you can cook the grain separately, and mix everything together before serving. This prevents over-cooking or under-cooking different components of the meal, depending on the grain cooking time.
3. Use a stock pot with a tight fitting lid.
4. Bring the correct amount of water to a boil, for the amount of grain you're preparing. Once the water boils, add the grain and reduce the heat. Check half-way through cooking to be sure there is enough water.
5. At the end of cooking time, taste the grains to be sure they're cooked enough for your preferences. Add more water and cook a bit longer if necessary.
6. Fluff them with a fork when cooking is done, so you don't get a solid mass. You can stir salt, herbs and spices in at this time.

RICE WITH CASHEWS AND COCONUT

This is a rich, filling recipe, perfect for teens with big appetites. You can add protein condiments, but it also works well accompanied by a high protein Indian-style lentil dish, such as the Dal recipe on page 62.

Basmati rice is idea for this recipe. I actually prefer to use short-grain brown rice, although it's hard to find in mainstream grocery stores. It's got a lovely chewy texture. Brown rice will also boost the fiber content significantly.

The flavor of the cashews is greatly enhanced by toasting them before use. If you can't find roasted unsalted cashews, buy plain unroasted ones and roast them in a 350 degree oven in a single layer on a cookie sheet for about 5 minutes. You don't want them getting very brown, and they will continue to toast on the pan after you take them out of the oven. You can roast lots of them ahead and keep unused nuts in the refrigerator.

Ingredients for 6 servings
- 2 cups basmati, white or brown rice of your choice
- 4 cups water
- 1 cup toasted unsalted cashews
- OPTIONAL: ½ tsp. black mustard seeds
- ½ tsp. turmeric
- 2 cloves garlic
- ½ cup flaked coconut
- 1 TB toasted sesame oil
- 1 TB peanut oil or other bland oil
- ¼ cup chopped fresh cilantro
- juice of ½ lemon or lime
- 1-2 TB minced jalapeno to taste
- salt to taste

Protein condiment options per serving:

o without added protein
425 calories • 9 gr protein • 23 gr fat • 53 g carbs • 4 gr fiber
o Vegans: 1 oz. tofu
440 calories • 10 gr protein • 24 gr fat • 53 g carbs • 4 gr fiber
o Vegetarians: 1 scrambled egg
500 calories • 16 gr protein • 27 gr fat • 53 g carbs • 4 gr fiber
o Meat eaters: 1 oz. cooked shrimp OR 1 oz. cooked chicken breast
460 calories • 16 gr protein • 23 gr fat • 53 g carbs • 4 gr fiber

Make the rice

1. Use pre-cooked rice, or cook 1-1/2 cups raw rice in 3 cups water (20 minutes for basmati; 45 minutes for brown rice), checking periodically to be sure there is enough water. Adjust water and cooking time to suit your preferences. When done, let it sit for a few minutes, then fluff with a fork. Alternatively, use a rice cooker and follow directions.
2. Mince the garlic. Separately, mince the cilantro.
3. Heat the peanut oil in a sauté pan. Add the black mustard seeds and cook briefly until they pop and turn gray.
4. Add the garlic and jalapeno and continue to sauté for 1-2 more minutes.
5. Add the sautéed garlic mixture to the rice.
6. Add the cashews, coconut, lemon juice, turmeric, sesame oil and cilantro to the rice and mix thoroughly. Add salt to taste.
7. Prepare the protein foods and serve them separately, to be mixed into the rice at the table.

Sides:

- This dish goes well with a lentil (dal) dish, which also boosts protein.
- Sautéed mixed vegetables, such as peppers, onion, broccoli, bok choy, greens, cauliflower
- Chopped vegetable salad, with tomato, scallions, cucumbers, minced fresh herbs, avocado. Boost the protein with grated cheese or chopped fresh mozzarella, crumbled soft tofu or toasted walnuts.
- A yogurt-based raita, which also adds protein.
- Sautéed garbanzo beans on page 66.

Types of Rice

Plain white rice can be used in any rice dish, and blends well with seasonings.

Basmati rice has a unique nutty flavor and is ideal for Indian-style curries. Brown basmati will have a slightly stronger flavor and chewier texture.

Brown rice is available in long, medium and short grain sizes. Long grain is widely available. Short grain brown rice is a delightful option, chewy and flavorful.

Jasmine rice is a good choice for Asian style dishes.

Arborio or carnaroli rice is the choice for risotto.

Some grocery stores now carry more exotic varieties, such as red and black rice. These have unique flavors, and go well with specific recipes.

Wild rice has a very strong flavor. It adds taste and visual interest to plain white rice. On it's own, it's best served as a side dish.

BARLEY WITH GREENS AND BEANS

Barley is a delicious and versatile grain, readily available in grocery stores. You can use it in soups or casseroles. It cooks in about 40 minutes, depending on your stove settings.

No barley? You can also make this with quinoa or short grain brown rice. If you want to be more adventurous, try farro, a whole grain that was a staple food in Italy centuries ago. It's related to wheat.

Although it's not officially soup, this one-pot recipe can be served in a bowl. It's high fiber, thanks to the barley and beans, and makes a very hearty and filling meal, great for a cold winter day.

Thanks to the combination of beans and barley this dish is already a good protein source. You could serve it without additional protein condiments.

Ingredients for 4 generous servings

- 1-1/2 cups pearl barley
- water and/or stock for cooking barley
- 1 bunch Swiss chard, or 1 bunch fresh spinach or 6-8 oz. frozen chopped spinach
- 1 15-oz can diced tomatoes
- 1 onion, chopped
- 2 carrots, peeled and chopped
- 2 stalks celery, chopped
- 1 cup sliced mushrooms
- 1 15-oz can white kidney beans, drained
- 2 cloves garlic, minced
- olive oil for the sauté pan
- 1 tsp. dried oregano
- ¼ tsp. dried thyme
- 1 tsp. ground fennel seeds
- salt and pepper to taste

Protein condiment options per serving:

o Vegans: 2 TB chopped toasted walnuts
565 calories • 20 gr protein • 17 gr fat • 89 g carbs • 21 gr fiber

o Vegetarians: ¼ cup grated Parmesan, Romano or other cheese
585 calories • 26 gr protein • 16 gr fat • 89 g carbs • 20 gr fiber

o Meat eaters: 2 oz. cooked lean pork, chicken, bison or beef. 1 slice crumbled bacon adds more flavor, although not much protein.
570 calories • 36 gr protein • 10 gr fat • 88 g carbs • 20 gr fiber

Make the Barley

1. Bring 4 cups water/stock to a boil. Gradually add the barley, reduce heat. Simmer, watching the pot to keep it from boiling over. Add more water towards the end of cooking if necessary. The barley should be slightly chewy.

2. Sauté the onion, carrot, celery, mushrooms, garlic and herbs in olive oil.

3. Wash, remove stems and roughly chop fresh greens if using. Add to the sautéed vegetables and cook briefly. If using frozen greens, add those towards the end of cooking.

4. Drain some of the liquid off the tomatoes and add to the vegetables.

5. Add the beans

6. Mix the barley gently into the vegetable/bean mixture.

7. Add salt and pepper to taste.

8. Warm leftover meat, if using, and serve separately at the table.

9. Serve walnuts and/or cheese at the table.

Sides:

- tossed green salad, add toasted nuts for extra protein if you are not adding protein condiments to the barley.
- raw vegetable sticks with hummus dip (extra protein for vegans)
- pita or French bread

RISOTTO

Risotto is a classic Italian rice dish. It's cooked differently from regular white or brown rice. Instead of simply boiling the water, adding the rice, putting the lid on and cooking for 20 or so minutes, you cook risotto by first sautéing rice, and then gradually adding the water, stock or wine in small batches, stirring with each addition, until it's done. It's a more hands-on process, so you need to be involved with the cooking for a half hour or more.

For risotto, buy rice suitable for this kind of dish: carnaroli or aborio are the common varieties available in grocery stores. The grains are plumper than regular white rice.

If you like a stronger flavor, sauté 1-2 cloves of minced garlic with the onions. However, risotto without garlic can be a lovely dish with a more subtle flavor.

Vegetables cooked in the risotto add color and a more flavor. Depending on the vegetables you include, risotto can become a convenient and filling one-pot meal. Best choices to accomplish that include spinach or other greens, peas, tomatoes or Brussels sprouts. But do experiment with other vegetables of your choice.

You can certainly make a very simple plain risotto, with just onion if you are serving vegetable side dishes or a tossed green salad.

Ingredients for 4 servings

- 1-1/2 cups risotto rice
- 1 cup chopped onion
- 3 TB olive oil
- 3-4 cups hot water and/or stock (1/2 to 1 cup of liquid can be white wine)
- vegetables, such as
  - 1-1/2 cups spinach (frozen chopped spinach is easiest) or other chopped fresh greens like chard, beet greens.
  - 2 cups sliced summer squash or zucchini
  - 1-1/2 cups peeled Butternut squash chunks
  - 1-1/2 cups green peas (frozen peas are easiest)
- salt, pepper, basil, oregano

Protein condiment options per serving:
- o Vegans: 3 TB chopped toasted pecans, pine nuts or walnuts
  570 calories • 11 gr protein • 27 gr fat • 75 g carbs • 7 gr fiber
- o Vegetarians: ¼ cup grated Parmesan or other hard grating cheese
  520 calories • 18 gr protein • 18 gr fat • 73 g carbs • 5 gr fiber
- o Meat eaters: 2 oz. cooked chicken, shrimp or turkey
  510 calories • 26 gr protein • 13 gr fat • 72 g carbs • 5 gr fiber

Make the risotto

1. Sauté the onion with the herbs briefly in the olive oil over medium heat in a 3 quart saucepan.
2. Add the dry rice grains and stir around a bit to coat with oil. Keep stirring for 2-3 minutes. You may need to add another TB of olive oil. Do not brown the rice.
3. Reduce heat slightly and start adding the liquid. If you're using wine, add it first, and stir the grains as the liquid is absorbed. Then add water or stock, 1/2 to 3/4 cup at a time, and stir the grains steadily while the liquid is absorbed.
4. After you've added about 2-1/2 cups of the liquid, taste a few rice grains to see how soft they are. Risotto shouldn't be cooked until it's mushy, but the finished rice texture is your decision. It can be a bit chewy, but definitely not crunchy.
5. If you're using butternut squash chunks, add them now, cover the pot and keep warm to the squash cooks until just tender, not mushy. Check the pot and add a bit more liquid if necessary to keep it from drying out.
6. For summer squash and fresh greens, sauté those briefly in a separate pan, and add to the risotto pan. If you're using frozen vegetables, simply add them to the risotto towards the end of cooking. They will cook in the hot rice.
7. If you aren't serving vegans, you can add 1/2 cup grated Parmesan to the rice.
8. *After* adding any cheese, salt the rice to taste and serve grated cheese at the table.
9. Serve the other protein add-ins at the table.

Sides:
- tossed green salad (add cheese or nuts for extra protein if you like)
- Sautéed eggplant/zucchini/peppers/tomatoes/onion/garlic
- fresh vegetable sticks (carrot, celery, cucumber radish)
- French or artisanal bread, for people who need more calories

---

Salad isn't always about greens

Tossed green salad is a great addition to almost any meal. Greens are healthy and delicious. But sometimes those salads get boring and repetitive. Enter the chunky vegetable salad.

There's no rule that defines "salad" as being made of greens. You can serve lots of different vegetable combinations cold, dressed with vinaigrette. The vegetables can be raw, or lightly steamed leftovers. Here are some combination ideas:

- Tomatoes, cucumbers, radishes, sweet peppers

- Broccoli, cauliflower, mushrooms

- Carrots, celery, radishes, purple cabbage

- Tomatoes, scallions, zucchini, , corn, avocado

- Sugar snap peas, carrots, broccoli, scallions

Let your vegetable preferences be your guide. Dress with oil, a splash of vinegar, salt, pepper and herbs of your choice.

POLENTA PIZZA CASSEROLE

Polenta is a traditional Italian dish made with finely ground corn. It's similar to grits, although a bit less gritty. Soft polenta has a texture more like hot cereal, while firm-cooked polenta has a more cake-like texture and can be cut into pieces.

Soft polenta can be served plain, as a side dish, or topped with a sauce or vegetables. Cheese can be mixed into the polenta or used as a topping. Polenta that is cooked to a firmer texture works well as the base of a casserole or even a polenta pizza.

Cooking polenta is easy, but some people may find it time-consuming or too much trouble. Fortunately, there's now an alternative to cooking. You can find pre-cooked, ready-to-use polenta in many grocery stores, in plastic tubes, called chubs. This makes a polenta-based dinner extremely easy to throw together in a hurry.

If you want to try cooking polenta from scratch, it's not hard to do, although it does take time. The good news is you can cook it ahead of time and reheat for your recipe. To cook soft polenta from scratch:

- Bring 3 cups water to a boil, and add 2 tsp. salt.
- As water boils, whisk 1 cup dry polenta into the water in a slow steady stream.
- Keep whisking to prevent lumps from forming.
- Once all the polenta meal is added, reduce heat and simmer for about 20 minutes, whisking every 2-3 minutes.
- You can also stir the polenta with a spoon or heat-proof spatula so it doesn't stick to the bottom of the pot.
- Add water as necessary to keep the mixture from sticking and drying out.

This recipe uses pre-cooked polenta, but you can substitute your own home-cooked if you like. It's a good way to make a gluten-free pizza.

Ingredients for 4 servings

- 1 18-oz chub ready-to-use polenta
- 1 bottle prepared meatless spaghetti sauce
- 4 cups mixed vegetables, such as mushrooms, onions, eggplant, zucchini, summer squash, sweet peppers.
- 3 TB olive oil
- OPTIONAL: ½ cup chopped black olives
- ¼ cup chopped fresh basil or 1 tsp. dried basil
- 2 cups grated mozzarella, if not serving vegans

Protein condiment options per serving:

o Vegans: 1 oz. soy cheese or soy sausage substitute
360 calories • 13 gr protein • 17 gr fat • 42 g carbs • 6 gr fiber

o Vegetarians: 1 oz. fresh mozzarella OR ¼ cup grated Parmesan or other hard grating cheese
370 calories • 14 gr protein • 18 gr fat • 41 g carbs • 6 gr fiber

o Meat eaters: 1 oz. cooked Italian sausage or cooked chicken
340 calories • 11 gr protein • 15 gr fat • 41 g carbs • 6 gr fiber

Make the polenta

1. Open the polenta and slice it into 10 even rounds (about 1/2 inch each). Arrange evenly in a greased shallow baking dish, either a 9-inch square or 6X10 rectangle
2. Press the polenta rounds out a bit so they blend together to cover the bottom of the pan evenly.
3. Sauté your chosen vegetables in olive oil, with dried basil.
4. Spread about 2 cups of the marinara sauce over the polenta.
5. If using fresh basil, mix into the sautéed vegetables, then spread the vegetables and olives (if using) over the top of the polenta.
6. If you aren't serving vegans, sprinkle the mozzarella over the vegetables.
7. Bake at 350 degrees until the sauce is bubbly and the cheese is melted, about 20-25 minutes.

Sides:

- Tossed green salad with olive oil vinaigrette. Add sunflower seeds to boost protein for vegans
- Chunky vegetable salad: tomato, cucumbers, radishes, green peppers, fresh peas
- Fresh fruit salad

TIP: You can use soft polenta to make a non-baked version of this recipe. Add enough water to the hot polenta to make it the consistency of mashed potatoes. Add the mozzarella or grated Parmesan to the hot polenta and stir until it melts. Mix fresh basil into the polenta, if using. Serve it in shallow bowls. Top with sauce, vegetables and additional cheese or meat of choice.

Soft polenta makes for an easy and delicious quick comfort food. If you're using pre-cooked polenta, put it in a large sauce pan and carefully add water, blending the polenta and water until smooth.

Add water until it's a consistency you like, somewhat like mashed potatoes. It should hold its shape on a plate. Season with salt and pepper, and herbs like basil, oregano and thyme.

You can mix cheese directly into the warmed polenta. Grated parmesan, soft feta, ricotta, mozzarella, Jack and cheddar are all good choices. Or put grated cheese on the polenta when serving.

You can top the polenta with a variety of cooked vegetables, or just serve a green salad on the side and enjoy the warm cheesy polenta by itself.

UNFRIED RICE

Everyone loves fried rice, but most commercial versions are just seasoned rice with a smattering of vegetables. The other problem is that it can be very high calorie from added oil.

This version is easy to make, emphasizes vegetables and limits the oil. Much healthier, very filling and able to stand on its own as an entrée.

If you've got leftover rice from some other meal, this is a great way to use it up. So if you're cooking rice as a side dish for another meal, make extra and serve up Unfried Rice for another dinner.

Ingredients for 4 servings
- 1-1/2 raw cups white rice (Jasmine is a good choice) or brown rice. Or use up 4 cups leftover cooked rice.
- 1-1/2 cups sliced green or Napa cabbage
- 1 medium onion, sliced
- 1-1/2 cups broccoli flowerets
- 1-1/2 cups whole sugar snap peas
- 1/2 cup sliced carrots
- 1/2 cup sliced celery
- 1-2 cloves garlic, minced
- 3 TB soy sauce or tamari, or to taste
- 1-2 TB rice wine vinegar (to taste)
- 2 TB peanut oil
- 1-1/2 TB toasted sesame oil
- 1 tsp. powdered ginger
- OPTIONAL: Sriracha sauce to taste

Protein condiment options per serving:

o Vegans: 2 TB chopped peanuts OR toasted sliced almonds or 2 oz. sautéed tofu chunks
580 calories • 15 gr protein • 22 gr fat • 84 g carbs • 10 gr fiber

o Vegetarians: 1 scrambled egg
565 calories • 17 gr protein • 20 gr fat • 81 g carbs • 8 gr fiber

o Meat eaters: 2 oz. shredded pork OR cooked chicken OR cooked shrimp
600 calories • 27 gr protein • 19 gr fat • 80 g carbs • 8 gr fiber

Make the rice

1. Bring 3 cups water to a boil. Add the rice and reduce heat. Simmer for 20 minutes until done (40 min for brown rice). If using a rice cooker, cook according to directions.
2. Prepare all the vegetables by chopping and slicing.
3. If you are using tofu, sauté slices in a separate pan in peanut oil until browned on both sides. Turn off heat and set aside.
4. If using scrambled egg, cook in a separate pan and set aside.
5. Put any other protein condiments into serving bowls.
6. Heat a large sauté pan or wok and coat with peanut oil. Add the prepared vegetables and garlic, and stir constantly to cook evenly and quickly. Don't over cook. The broccoli should still be bright green in color.
7. Add the cooked rice to the vegetables and toss to combine. Add the seasonings and stir to incorporate, keeping the pan on low heat.
8. Adjust the seasonings according to your preferences.

Sides:
- Sliced cucumber salad
- Fruit salad, fresh berries or melon slices

QUINOA SUMMER SALAD

This recipe is adapted from one that uses black rice (Forbidden Rice). It's delicious, but many people won't be able to find pricey black rice in the grocery store, or won't be able to convince their kids to eat it. Quinoa boosts the protein content considerably. If you aren't using it, I recommend using brown rice. If you can find black rice, and don't mind experimenting or the extra cost, it's worth a try.

This salad is filling, thanks to the raw vegetables. The avocado adds fat, so you don't need so much oil for the dressing. If you're serving vegans and want to boost the protein in the meal, serve a bean salad as a side dish.

Ingredients for 4 servings
- 1-1/2 cups quinoa.
- 2 TB peanut or canola oil
- 2 cups fresh sugar snap peas, sliced in half
- 1 avocado, chopped
- 2 cups chopped fresh tomato
- ½ cup sliced scallions
- juice of one lime
- ¼ tsp. cayenne pepper (or to taste)
- salt to taste
- ¼ cup chopped fresh mint leaves

Protein condiment options per serving:
- o Vegans: 2 oz. crumbled soft tofu OR 2 TB pine nuts or chopped walnuts
  440 calories • 16 gr protein • 19 gr fat • 54 g carbs • 11 gr fiber
- o Vegetarians: 2 oz. crumbled low fat feta OR goat cheese
  530 calories • 24 gr protein • 25 gr fat • 55 g carbs • 12 gr fiber
- o Meat eaters: 2 oz. canned albacore tuna or chicken
  480 calories • 26 gr protein • 20 gr fat • 53 g carbs • 10 gr fiber

Make the salad

1. Cook the quinoa according to package instructions. If using brown or white rice, bring 3 cups water to a boil, add rice, reduce heat and simmer 40 minutes (brown) or 20 minutes (white).
2. Transfer the cooked quinoa to a large mixing bowl to cool to room temperature, fluffing it with a fork every 5-10 minutes to prevent clumping.
3. When the quinoa is cooled to room temperature, add the oil and mix thoroughly. Refrigerate.
4. Prep the peas, tomato, avocado and scallions and add to the bowl of quinoa.
5. Add the lime juice, chopped mint, salt and cayenne to taste, and mix everything thoroughly.
6. Adjust the seasonings to your preference before serving with the protein condiments.
7. You can make this salad ahead and refrigerate before serving.

Sides:
- corn on the cob
- crusty artisanal whole grain bread
- warmed tortillas with refried beans, melted cheese (except for vegans) and salsa.
- Bean salad (page 46), which boosts protein.

TABOULI

Tabouli (or Tabbouleh) is a traditional Middle Eastern salad dish with as many variations as cooks. Traditionally it's made with bulgur wheat, although some recipes use couscous. Fresh chopped mint is an essential ingredient, giving tabouli a delightful refreshing flavor.

This recipe doesn't have particular protein condiments. It's strictly meatless. Add garbanzo beans for a protein boost. Or serve higher protein side dishes, such as Sautéed Garbanzo beans, Mukimame Salad, cooked edamame or hummus. You can serve the meat eaters grilled chicken. Vegetarians might add some crumbled feta cheese to a side salad, or have fresh mozzarella, tomatoes and basil.

I prefer to use cracked bulgur rather than whole bulgur wheat grains when making this recipe. This is a make-ahead recipe, perfect for a weekend meal, when you have time early in the day to assemble it.

Ingredients for 6 servings
- 2 cups raw bulgur wheat
- 2-1/2 cups boiling hot water
- 2 large cucumbers, peeled, seeded and chopped (about 4 cups)
- 3-4 cups chopped fresh tomatoes. Halved cherry tomatoes work well.
- ½ to 1 cup chopped fresh mint (to taste)
- 1 bunch scallions, minced
- juice of 2 lemons
- ½ cup olive oil
- 1-1/2 tsp. salt
- pepper to taste
- 1 can garbanzo beans, drained and rinsed

420 calories • 11 gr protein • 20 gr fat • 55 g carbs • 12 gr fiber

Make the tabouli

1. Put the raw bulgur in a large bowl. Pour the boiling water over it. Let stand until room temperature.
2. Sprinkle the mint over the bulgur.
3. Layer the chopped cucumbers, chopped tomatoes and scallions over the bulgur.
4. Mix the lemon juice, olive oil and salt and pour over the bowl.
5. Cover with a plate directly onto the vegetable layer.
6. Cover the bowl with plastic wrap and refrigerate for 4 or more hours before serving.
7. At serving time, stir everything together and mix in the garbanzo beans (if using).
8. Add more salt, mint or lemon juice, according to your taste.

Sides:
- Hummus and pita bread
- Mukimame salad
- Salad of mixed baby greens with pecans/walnuts and feta cheese
- For meat eaters: grilled chicken

NOODLE DISHES

The busy parent will be relieved to know that many noodle-based dishes already popular with kids and teens are vegetarian by default. So unless you're feeding a vegan, you may already have a repertoire of meatless dishes:

- Macaroni and cheese
- Meatless lasagna
- Spaghetti and marinara sauce with grated cheese (omit the grated cheese and this is the only one that can be vegan)
- Cheese ravioli

All perfectly fine entrees. Serve with a tossed green salad and you've got dinner. There are plenty of recipes for those on the Internet. You may have your own favorite recipes.

Noodles have been around for hundreds of years. In addition to the familiar pasta noodles, there are egg noodles, buckwheat noodles, rice noodles and many newer gluten free noodles, made from corn or other alternative grains. Wheat noodles are the most common because they hold together best. Noodles made with corn or alternative grains can be more fragile, and require less cooking time. When using those, *always* consult the cooking directions on the package. In some cases, the noodles aren't cooked at all; rather they're soaked in hot water and then drained.

VEGAN-IZE THESE RECIPES

Cheese is an essential part of Italian-style pasta dishes. It provides flavor and texture, and melts nicely. Tofu may look a bit like cheese, but it has little flavor and does not melt. Substituting it in a dish like lasagna will produce a very different result, which may not be to everyone's liking.

Tofu and cheese have one thing in common: they're high protein. So using tofu in, say, a lasagna recipe will boost the protein, but alter the flavor and texture. One possible solution: increase the other flavor ingredients, such as garlic and herbs. Add some flavorful sautéed vegetables to the marinara, such as mushrooms, onions and peppers.

You can make a mac-and-cheese-like dish using soy milk for the sauce, but of course you can't use cheese. Again, you'll need to boost the flavor with herbs and spices. If you're not opposed to soy bacon bits, a sprinkling of those in the sauce will boost flavor.

Another way to boost flavor, whether in marinara or creamy sauce: sprinkle some ground toasted nuts, such as walnuts, over one of the layers.

SOBA (BUCKWHEAT) NOODLES

Soba, or buckwheat, noodles are used in Japanese cooking. The flat noodles are a deep brown color, and have a nutty flavor that blends well with mild flavors like tofu, chicken and fish. They're available in major grocery stores, in the Asian foods section.

Peanuts add lots of flavor, as well as some protein for everyone. Vegans and vegetarians may choose to add more, as tofu, or just stick to peanuts.

Ingredients for 6 servings
- 1 12-oz package Soba noodles
- 1 red pepper, sliced
- 3 cups green vegetables: broccoli flowerets or sugar snap peas
- 2 TB peanut oil or canola oil
- ½ cup sliced scallions
- ½ cup shredded carrot
- 2 TB soy sauce or tamari
- 1 TB toasted sesame oil
- ¼ tsp. crushed red pepper flakes
- 1 tsp. ginger
- ½ cup roasted unsalted peanuts, chopped

Protein condiment options per serving:
- Vegans and Vegetarians: 2 oz. tofu
  440 calories • 18 gr protein • 19 gr fat • 51 g carbs • 6 gr fiber
- Meat eaters: 2 oz. chicken OR shrimp or other cooked fish
  490 calories • 31 gr protein • 19 gr fat • 50 g carbs • 6 gr fiber

Make the soba noodles

1. Cook the soba noodles according to package instructions. Typically they are boiled in salted water, like other pasta noodles, but for a shorter amount of time. *Do not over cook them, as they will fall apart.* Alternatively, you can soak them in hot water (check package directions). Drain the noodles, return to the pot and toss briefly with a drizzle of peanut oil.
2. In a small bowl, whisk together the sesame oil, soy sauce, ginger and pepper flakes.
3. Sauté the red pepper and broccoli/peas in a hot sauté pan brushed with peanut oil. Do not overcook. The vegetables should have bright color and remain a bit crunchy.
4. If using tofu, cut into slices or cubes. Sauté briefly to brown, if you prefer.
5. If serving chicken/fish, cook ahead or cut left overs into bite sized pieces.
6. Toss the noodles with sesame oil mixture, shredded carrots and scallions. Add the broccoli and mix together gently.
7. Garnish with chopped peanuts when serving, adding other protein foods at the table, if using.

Sides:
- Cabbage slaw dressed with oil and vinegar
- Sushi (such as packaged sushi available in many grocery stores)
- Sautéed mixed greens, such as chard, spinach or kale with garlic.

MEDITERRANEAN COUSCOUS

Couscous is a *noodle*? Sure looks like a grain. But yes, despite the grain-like appearance, couscous is not a grain. There is no couscous plant. But it is made from wheat. It's a popular food in the Mediterranean regions, especially in North African countries.

The most common variety of couscous in grocery stores comes in tiny pieces, like grains of sand, which cook *very* quickly. Israeli couscous comes in larger pearl-sized pieces, which are boiled in water like any other pasta, to al dente firmness. You can use either one in this recipe. The Israeli variety is harder to find at grocery stores, but it usually available in specialty groceries. Either type works well as a hot dish, or cold for summer salads. Orzo – a small grain-sized pasta -- also works well for this dish. It's sold in boxes at most grocery stores.

You can serve this dish hot or cold. If you're going to serve it as a cold entrée for hot weather, use fresh basil, raw tomatoes, chopped cucumber and scallions rather than dried basil, canned tomatoes and sautéed onion. Shrimp, garbanzo beans and crumbled feta work best for salad. The mint adds a refreshing flavor when serving this cold.

Ingredients for 4 servings
- 1-1/2 cups couscous
- 2 cups water
- 1 15-oz can diced tomatoes
- 3 TB olive oil
- ¾ cup chopped onion
- 1 green pepper, chopped
- 1 tsp. basil or 2 TB fresh basil, minced
- 1 tsp. oregano
- juice of ½ lemon, or to taste
- optional: grated zest of ½ lemon
- optional (recommended): 2 TB chopped fresh mint

Protein condiment options per serving:

o Vegans: 2 TB toasted walnuts or pine nuts AND/OR ¼ cup garbanzo beans
   475 calories • 12 gr protein • 21 gr fat • 62 g carbs • 5 gr fiber

o Vegetarians: 2 oz. fresh mozzarella OR feta cheese
   520 calories • 20 gr protein • 22 gr fat • 62 g carbs • 4 gr fiber

o Meat eaters: 2 oz. cooked ground lamb OR cooked shrimp
   540 calories • 24 gr protein • 19 gr fat • 60 g carbs • 4 gr fiber

Make the couscous

1. Cook the couscous according to package instructions. If no instructions, bring 2 cups of water to a boil in a saucepan. Add the dry couscous, stir briefly, cover and turn off the heat. Let the pan sit for 5 minutes, to allow the couscous to absorb the water. When the water is absorbed, fluff the couscous with a fork.

2. In a separate sauté pan, heat the olive oil and sauté the onion, green pepper and herbs over moderate heat until the vegetables are soft. This takes about 5 minutes.

3. Prepare the protein foods you will be using: toast walnuts, drain and rinse a can of garbanzo beans, cook ground lamb or shrimp.

4. Add lemon juice, lemon zest and canned tomatoes to the sauté pan.

5. Add the cooked couscous to the vegetables in the sauté pan and stir gently to mix, but avoid mashing the couscous.

6. Add salt and pepper to taste, and chopped mint, if using

7. If everyone will enjoy the walnuts and/or garbanzo beans, add those before serving.

8. If using grated cheese or cooked lamb or shrimp, add those at the table to individual servings.

Sides:
- French bread, ciabatta, focaccia or other bread
- Roasted or grilled vegetables
- Boost protein with a bean dish or bean salad

Couscous salad option:

After fluffing the cooked couscous, put it in a large mixing bowl and add olive oil.

Stir again, gently, and allow to cool.

Meanwhile prepare 1-1/2 cups chopped fresh tomatoes, 1 sliced cucumber, 1 chopped green pepper and 4-5 sliced scallions

Mince 1-2 TB fresh basil and mint.

Add vegetables and herbs to the couscous and stir briefly.

Add any protein foods that everyone will eat such as walnuts, garbanzo beans or crumbled feta.

Add lemon juice to taste, and more olive oil if necessary. Season with salt and pepper.

Which breads to serve?

Should you be serving nothing but whole wheat bread with dinner? The official nutrition mantra of "eat whole grains" implies that anything other than whole wheat bread is an unhealthy mistake.

Bread is served at meals in many countries. It makes the meal more filling and provides variety. For active growing teens, bread can provide extra calories and nutrients.

Certainly if your teens enjoy whole (or partially whole) grain breads, serve those. The point should be to serve bread that tastes great. Sometimes that means a non-whole-grain crusty French baguette or Italian ciabatta or artisanal loaf from a local bakery.

If all you eat is one piece of bread, switching to a whole grain bread isn't going to make a huge difference in nutrient intake. It makes more sense to enjoy whole grain breads when bread is a key part of the meal: for morning toast or for sandwiches.

So serve whole grain breads with dinner if (1) your family enjoys them and (2) your teens can use the extra calories.

PAD THAI-STYLE RICE NOODLES

Pad Thai is a great and versatile South East Asian dish that's easy to adapt to your own preferences. It's also very easy to make it meatless. Traditionally it has chopped peanuts, which are OK for everyone. Vegans can substitute crumbled soft tofu for the shrimp. Some recipes call for pieces of scrambled egg, which would work for vegetarians and meat eaters alike.

If you can't find special pad Thai noodles, just use regular fettuccini or linguini. Not quite the same, but acceptable. Lo Mein noodles also work.

NOTE: the seasonings should all be adjusted to your own taste preferences.

Ingredients for 4 servings
- 12 oz. Pad Thai noodles (wide rice noodles)
- ¼ cup soy sauce, more to taste
- 1 TB hoisin sauce
- 3 TB peanut oil
- 1 TB chile garlic paste
- 2 tsp. minced garlic
- 1 jalapeno, minced fine
- ½ cup roughly chopped unsalted roasted peanuts
- ¼ cup fish sauce. If this is not be acceptable to the vegans, offer it at the table as a condiment for non-vegans.
- ½ cup chopped scallions
- 2/3 cup chopped fresh cilantro
- 1 lime cut into wedges
- Optional condiment: fresh bean sprouts, such as mung beans. You can find these in the refrigerated produce section, typically in plastic bags or packages. Some stores do not carry sprouts anymore due to problems with spoilage. If you buy sprouts, check the expiration date on the package and use them right away.

Protein condiment options per serving:
- o   Vegans: 2 oz. tofu cubes
  545 calories • 17 gr protein • 22 gr fat • 72 g carbs • 4 gr fiber
- o   Vegetarians: 1 scrambled egg
  570 calories • 19 gr protein • 24 gr fat • 72 g carbs • 3 gr fiber
- o   Meat eaters: 2 oz. cooked shrimp
  550 calories • 25 gr protein • 20 gr fat • 71 g carbs • 3 gr fiber

Make the Pad Thai

1. Soak the Pad Thai noodles in hot water for 15-20 minutes, until they are softened. Follow package directions for more information. Drain.
2. Whisk together the soy sauce, chile paste, garlic, hoisin and fish sauce (if using) in a small bowl.
3. Cook the shrimp, if they are not pre-cooked, by simmering in hot water until pink, 2-3 minutes. Drain and set aside. Alternatively, shrimp can be grilled on skewers.
4. Heat a wok or large frying pan over high heat, add the oil.
5. Quickly add the minced jalapeno and spice mixture and stir for one minute.
6. Add the drained noodles and scallions and stir-fry briefly to heat through and coat the noodles, stirring constantly.
7. Turn off the heat. Add the bean sprouts, if you are using them, and mix in.
8. Each person can garnish their noodles with cilantro, peanuts, lime wedges and protein foods at the table.

Sides:
- ▪ Vegetables in coconut curry sauce
- ▪ Fresh fruit, such as melon slices
- ▪ Stir-fried ginger vegetables: broccoli, snap peas, red pepper and onion

VEGETABLE PASTA VARIATIONS

There's no law that says you *have* to put tomato sauce on pasta. Sometimes you just need a change. Tossing pasta with a mixture of sautéed vegetables and garnishing with herbs, nuts, cheese or meat is a really easy and delicious way to serve noodles.

This recipe gives you endless options for combining vegetables. It's a good way to use up vegetables that need to be used up. You can invent your own combinations, but here are some suggestions:
- Broccoli, cauliflower and mushrooms
- Zucchini and tomatoes
- Sugar snap peas and peppers
- Eggplant, peppers, zucchini and tomatoes
- Greens and mushrooms

Ingredients for 6 servings
- One pound package of fettuccini or linguini
- ¼ cup olive oil
- 6+ cups of your choice of raw chopped vegetables:
    o sliced sweet peppers
    o eggplant cubes
    o sliced zucchini or summer squash
    o fresh tomatoes
    o mushrooms
    o broccoli or cauliflower flowerets
    o sugar snap peas
    o fresh spinach or chard
- chopped onion
- 2-3 cloves garlic, minced
- OPTIONAL: if not using fresh tomatoes, 1/3 cup minced sundried tomatoes
- 1 TB dried basil
- 1 tsp. dried oregano

Protein condiment options per serving:
- o Vegans: 2 TB toasted walnuts, sunflower seeds or pecans; (soynuts boost protein considerably)

  470 calories • 14 gr protein • 20 gr fat • 65 g carbs • 6 gr fiber
- o Vegetarians: 1 oz. grated cheese, such as Parmesan or mozzarella; fresh mozzarella cut into chunks

  490 calories • 21 gr protein • 18 gr fat • 64 g carbs • 5 gr fiber
- o Meat eaters: 2 oz. cooked meat or fish such as chicken, beef, shrimp

  475 calories • 29 gr protein • 13 gr fat • 63 g carbs • 5 gr fiber

Make the pasta

1. Cook the pasta in boiling salted water according to package instructions and your preferences for done-ness. Drain and return the noodles to the pot, toss with 2 TB of olive oil.
2. Chop the vegetables and sauté in remaining olive oil with garlic, onion and herbs.
3. Add the cooked vegetables to the pasta and mix gently to combine.
4. Serve protein condiments at the table

Sides:
- Tossed green salad
- French or Italian artisanal bread
- Bruschetta
- Depending on which vegetables you use in the pasta, serve a chunky vegetable salad using contrasting vegetables. For example, if you used mushrooms and broccoli, serve a simple cucumber tomato salad and garnish with fresh mozzarella or walnuts.
- Sautéed and glazed green beans or carrots

PUMPED UP RAMEN

Ramen has a reputation as a cheap, quick survival food for college students and people on a budget. Most of the taste comes from the little flavor packets.

That doesn't mean ramen can't be healthy. It's basically just noodles, a good basis for a meal, not the whole meal. The nutrition is easily pumped up with other ingredients. This recipe does just that, with the added benefit of being quick. Even a kitchen-phobic teenager can manage to make this dish.

One of the keys to making this taste special is using flavorful broth, not just water, to cook the ramen. There are several brands of quality vegetarian broth available in grocery stores now, but you can easily make your own, using the guidelines on page 50.

Ingredients for 4 servings
- 2 packages ramen, throw away the flavor packets
- 6 cups good quality vegetarian broth
- 2 tsp. minced garlic
- 1 TB peanut or canola oil
- ½ tsp. ginger or 2 tsp. minced fresh ginger
- 3 cups packed fresh spinach leaves or 2 cups (about 6 oz.) chopped frozen spinach
- 1 medium onion, chopped
- 1-2 TB toasted sesame oil
- ½ cup chopped scallions
- sprigs of fresh cilantro for garnish
- Sriracha to taste

Protein condiment options per serving:
- Vegans: 2 oz. firm tofu, sliced thin
  355 calories • 10 gr protein • 18 gr fat • 37 g carbs • 3 gr fiber
- Vegetarians and meat eaters: 1(or 2) eggs per person
  375 calories • 12 gr protein • 20 gr fat • 36 g carbs • 3 gr fiber

Make the ramen:

1. Heat a large soup pot or medium heat and sauté the chopped onion in the peanut or canola oil until soft, 2-3 minutes.
2. Add the broth, garlic and fresh ginger (if using) and frozen spinach (if using) and heat to a boil.
3. Add the dried ramen noodles and fresh spinach (if using) and simmer for 1-2 minutes, stirring constantly with a fork to break up the noodles.
4. Turn off the heat.
5. If using eggs, crack them directly into the soup pot. Cover the pot and let the eggs poach in the warm stock. They are done when the whites are set. It will take 3-4 minutes, depending on how hot the water is.
6. Use a slotted spoon to dish out the eggs into serving bowls. If using tofu, put slices into serving bowls.
7. Dish the rest of the soup into the bowls.
8. Drizzle a teaspoon of sesame oil over each bowl.
9. Garnish with scallions and cilantro to taste.
10. Use Sriracha as a condiment.

Sides:
- Fresh fruit or fruit salad
- Edamame salad
- Baked or pan-fried Asian dumplings or pot stickers (frozen in grocery store)

PASTA SALAD

If you think pasta salad means macaroni doused with mayonnaise, think again. Pasta salads can be extremely versatile and seasonal. You could theoretically eat pasta salad every night and never eat the same thing twice in a week.

When making pasta salad, take advantage of fresh seasonal vegetables. There are plenty of suggestions in this recipe, but feel free to add your own favorites. The more vegetables, the better.

What about that mayonnaise? The recipe calls for olive oil, but you can substitute half as mayonnaise if you like that flavor.

Ingredients for roughly 4 servings
- One pound package macaroni, rotini, penne, shells or other small pasta
- ¼-1/3 cup olive oil (optional: canola oil)
- juice from one lemon (about 3 TB)
- ¼ cup chopped fresh basil
- ½ cup chopped scallions
- OPTIONAL: 2 TB minced fresh oregano
- 4 cups of your choice of a mix of chopped raw vegetables, such as tomatoes, cucumbers, carrots, sweet peppers, radishes, zucchini, snap peas or fresh shelled peas
- one 15-oz can garbanzo beans
- salt and pepper to taste
- OPTIONAL: one avocado, cut into ½ inch chunks

Protein condiment options per serving:

o   Vegans: chopped walnuts, pine nuts or pecans
    calories • gr protein • gr fat • g carbs • gr fiber

o   Vegetarians: grated hard cheese, such as Parmesan or Manchego OR fresh mozzarella or feta or goat cheese AND/OR chopped hard boiled egg

o   calories • gr protein • gr fat • g carbs • gr fiber

o   Meat eaters: cooked chicken OR turkey OR beef OR tuna OR shrimp OR cooked/smoked salmon
    calories • gr protein • gr fat • g carbs • gr fiber

Make the salad

1. Boil the pasta in water until done to your preference. Don't overcook or the pasta salad will be mushy.
2. Rinse the pasta in cold water and drain. Transfer to a large bowl and toss with the olive oil.
3. Chop your vegetables and fresh herbs
4. Drain and rinse the garbanzo beans
5. Mix everything together in the bowl, adding salt and pepper to taste. Add more lemon juice if you like.
6. If everyone is fine with nuts, mix those into the salad, and serve additional at the table for vegans

Sides:

- Crusty artisanal bread
- Greens: serve the pasta salad on a bed of Romaine or dark leaf lettuce, or arugula or fresh spinach
- Corn on the cob
- Grilled vegetables like eggplant, zucchini or onions

POTATOES AND MORE

Potatoes and other vegetables may not be high protein, but that doesn't mean they aren't highly nutritious. They're also filling, always a plus when it comes to hungry teenagers.

You can easily build a meal around potatoes, or other similar vegetables, and add high protein condiments to round out the nutrition. This is especially easy if you're feeding vegetarians. Who doesn't like cheese on potatoes? If cheese, yogurt and milk are on the menu, then turning vegetables into dinner is a whole lot easier.

But don't despair if your teen is a vegan. After all, vegan is about vegetables. Protein can be added in a variety of ways:

- Adding protein condiments, such as nuts, soy meat substitutes, soy "cheese", tofu or quinoa
- Adding servings of protein foods like soy burgers or alternate meats
- Making sure your teen is drinking soy milk, or a beverage fortified with plant-based protein, so it's equivalent to cow's milk protein content.

Pancakes or waffles might seem like an unusual choice for dinner, but there's no law that says you can't serve them. Instead of topping with sugary syrups, use applesauce, yogurt or fresh berries.

Potatoes originated in South America, and are now included in a variety of cuisines around the globe, from Europe to India and beyond.

Potatoes are highly nutritious and filling. They're a significant source of:

- Fiber

- Potassium

- Vitamin C

- Iron

- Other vitamins and minerals

Plus: low sodium and low fat.

CHEESE POTATO BAKE

This vegetarian recipe is easy and filling. Easy because you don't need to cook the potatoes ahead of time. Filling because potatoes are filling. If you've got the time, you can put it together in the morning, refrigerate and bake later for dinner.

If you have leftover cooked potatoes, it's a good way to use them up. You can reduce cooking time to 25-30 minutes.

This casserole doesn't work well as a one-pot meal. To balance out the meal, you need to serve sides that include green vegetables. See the suggestions below for some ideas.

Ingredients for 4 generous servings
- 5-6 medium potatoes, or about 2 lbs. of raw potatoes (sizes will vary). Yukon Gold or Russets are fine. You could be trendy, and use purple potatoes for an interesting color combination
- 2 cups grated cheese of your choice. Cheddar is great, but Swiss, Jack or Gruyere can also work
- 2 cups milk
- 2 tsp. salt
- Pinch of cayenne pepper
- 1 tsp. dried dill weed or rosemary

450 calories • 23 gr protein • 21 gr fat • 46 g carbs • 3 gr fiber

Make the casserole

1. Coat the bottom and sides of a 13 X 9 (or equivalent) pan with oil
2. Whisk the milk with the salt, cayenne and herb of choice.
3. Wash the potatoes and slice into thin rounds, about 1/8 inch thick.
4. Divide the potatoes into 3 equal piles. Layer one pile along the bottom of the pan, overlapping slices as necessary.
5. Sprinkle 1/3 of the cheese over the potatoes
6. Repeat for 2 more layers of potato and cheese, ending with cheese on the top.
7. Pour the milk over the casserole.
8. Bake at 350 until a fork goes easily into the potato layers, about 45 minutes. You may need to cover the casserole with aluminum foil towards the end of baking if the top is getting too brown.

Sides:
- Tossed green salad or other chopped vegetable salad.
- Simple steamed broccoli or green beans
- Roasted Brussels sprouts
- Sauté of greens, such as spinach, chard or beet greens
- Raw vegetable sticks: carrots, celery, radishes, broccoli, cucumbers, and green peppers.

STUFFED BAKED POTATOES

Stuffed potatoes can work for everyone, not just vegetarians. They're filling and tasty. You can garnish them with extra chopped vegetables (try black olives or minced sun dried tomatoes) or bacon or soy bacon.

Ingredients for 8 stuffed halves
- 4 Russet potatoes (about 3 X 5 inch or)
- 2 cups grated cheese, such as Cheddar, Swiss, Jack.
- 1 cup milk
- 4 TB minced fresh chives OR ½ tsp. dried dill weed
- salt and pepper to taste

275 calories • 12 gr protein • 10 gr fat • 35 g carbs • 2 gr fiber

Make the stuffed potatoes
1. Wash the potatoes, poke with a fork once or twice and bake at 350° until done, 45-60 minutes, depending on potato size.
2. Let the potatoes cool for about 15 minutes. Then slice in half lengthwise.
3. Scoop the cooked potato flesh from each half into a bowl, leaving ¼ to ½ inch of potato attached to the skin, to make a little potato bowl.
4. Mash the potato in the bowl with a fork, adding the milk and grated cheese, salt and herbs
5. Stuff the mashed potato mixture back into the potato skins.
6. Sprinkle with remaining cheese.
7. Arrange the potatoes in a shallow baking dish, cover loosely with foil and reheat until cheese melts and filling is hot.

Boost the protein in this meal by garnishing the potatoes with a dollop of plain Greek style yoghurt in place of sour cream.

Balance out the meal with green vegetable side dishes that have some crunch, to contrast with the potatoes:

- Raw vegetable sticks with a plain yogurt-based dip
- A simple steamed vegetable, like green beans or broccoli
- Roasted Brussels sprouts with pecans
- Tossed green salad with protein foods like grated cheese or nuts
- Chopped vegetable salad with radishes, cucumbers, peppers, tomatoes, scallions and vinaigrette dressing
- Stir-fried sugar snap peas and mushrooms

BLACK BEAN STUFFED SWEET POTATOES

Beans and potatoes? Sounds unusual. But in fact, if you've ever eaten a breakfast burrito, with refried beans and sautéed potatoes, you've eaten beans and potatoes together.

Both black beans and sweet potatoes work especially well with chili-type seasonings. There are many recipes on the Internet for sweet potato black bean chili. This stuffed potato recipe is a variation on that theme.

Sweet potatoes and yams come in a variety of sizes. A potato that's roughly 7 inches long and 3 inches across weighs almost a pound. That's probably enough for 2 people, so plan accordingly when you purchase potatoes.

Ingredients for 4 servings
- 2-3 lbs. sweet potatoes, which will likely be 2-3 large potatoes.
- Two 15-oz cans black beans, drained (about 3 cups beans)
- One 15-oz can diced tomatoes
- 1 cup roasted mild green chiles (from fresh, or canned)
- 1 TB corn or peanut oil
- ½ cup minced onion
- 1-2 tsp. minced fresh garlic, to taste
- ½ tsp. cumin
- 1 tsp. ground coriander
- 1 tsp. dried oregano
- 2 tsp. ground Chile rojo (not chili powder mix) or to taste
- juice from ½ lime
- salt to taste (for the beans)
- OPTIONAL: 1 TB minced fresh jalapeno, or to taste; ½ tsp. ground chipotle powder

¼ cup minced fresh cilantro.

Protein condiment options per serving:
o Vegans: 1 oz. crumbled soft tofu and 1 TB toasted sesame seeds or chopped toasted pecans
   560 calories • 20 gr protein • 14 gr fat • 89 g carbs • 19 gr fiber
o Vegetarians: 1 oz. grated Jack cheese
o 600 calories • 23 gr protein • 17 gr fat • 87 g carbs • 18 gr fiber
o Meat eaters: 2 oz. cooked chicken or turkey
   585 calories • 34 gr protein • 10 gr fat • 87 g carbs • 18 gr fiber

Make the stuffed sweet potatoes

1. Wash the potatoes and slice lengthwise down the middle about ½ inch deep, depending on the potato. Bake in a 350° oven for 30-40 minutes until fork-tender. They should still be firm enough to hold their shape.
2. Remove potatoes and allow to cool enough so you can handle them.
3. In a large sauce pan, sauté the onion, jalapeno (if using) and garlic over moderate heat in oil for 2 minutes. Add the oregano and spices at the end of cooking, as the onions get soft.
4. Drain the canned beans. Put beans from one can in a bowl and mash slightly with a fork.
5. Add the diced chiles, tomatoes and beans to the onions. Heat to a simmer and add salt to taste. Adjust seasoning to your taste preferences.
6. Add the lime juice and cilantro and turn off heat.
7. Using a soup spoon or medium serving spoon, scoop out the insides of the potatoes onto a cutting board, making potato boats, leaving at least ¾ inch of potato on the inside of the skin.
8. Chunk up the potato you removed with a knife. Add them to the bean mixture. Adjust seasonings if necessary.

9. Spoon bean stuffing into the potato boats until they're full, rounded on the top. You can layer the soft tofu or chicken/turkey pieces with the beans in individual potatoes.

10. Put the potatoes on a baking sheet and cover loosely with foil. Bake until heated through for another 15-20 minutes until the potatoes are fork-tender and the stuffing is bubbling.

11. Turn off oven. Top the stuffing with grated cheese (except for vegans) and allow cheese to melt before serving, about 2 minutes.

12. Garnish with sour cream or plain Greek style yoghurt.

Sides:
- Fresh fruit salad
- Corn avocado tomato salad
- Warmed tortillas
- Tossed green salad

SWEET POTATO CHILI VARIATION

The filling for the potatoes can also be served as a chili, with a slight cooking change.

1. Bake the potatoes until barely tender.
2. Remove from oven and allow to cool.
3. Meanwhile make the black bean mixture, according to directions above, except don't drain off all the liquid from the canned beans and don't mash the beans.
4. When potatoes are cooled off, remove skin and cut into 1-inch chunks
5. Add to chili and continue to simmer until potato pieces are cooked through.

Protein condiment options per serving:
o   **Vegans: 1-2 oz. crumbled soft tofu AND/OR 1 TB sesame seeds**
     calories • gr protein • gr fat • g carbs • gr fiber
o   **Vegetarians: 2 oz. grated Jack cheese**
o   calories • gr protein • gr fat • g carbs • gr fiber
o   **Meat eaters: 2 oz. cooked chicken or turkey**
     calories • gr protein • gr fat • g carbs • gr fiber

POTATO PANCAKES

Serving pancakes for a family meal may seem time consuming. While you're busy cooking the pancakes, everyone else eats them up as soon as they come off the pan. One way to solve this logistical problem is to cook them all ahead, and keep warm in the oven on a plate.

Another solution is to have your teen do the cooking. Pancakes are pretty easy, so this is a good practice opportunity for a new cook.

Boost protein in this meal by garnishing the pancakes with plain Greek style yogurt. Serving high protein sides, such as deviled eggs or grated cheese on a salad, also increases protein.

Ingredients for about 15 small cakes
- 5 medium baking potatoes (about 2-1/2 lbs.), washed and peeled
- ½ cup finely minced onion
- OPTIONAL: ¼ cup chopped fresh chives
- 2 eggs
- 2 cups grated cheese, such as Jack, Colby or Cheddar. Pepper Jack adds flavor.
- ¼ cup flour
- 1-1/2 to 2 teaspoons salt
- ¼ tsp. black pepper
- peanut or corn oil
- Garnishes: plain Greek style yogurt, salsa, pesto, chopped olives

Per pancake:
140 calories • 7 gr protein • 7 gr fat • 13 g carbs • 1 gr fiber

Fat and calories will vary according to how much oil is used for cooking, and how much drains off onto paper towels after cooking.

Make the pancakes

1. Beat the eggs in a large bowl. Set aside.
2. Grate the potatoes into a bowl. Take one handful at a time and squeeze out as much water as possible. Put the squeezed potatoes into the bowl with the eggs.
3. Add the flour, onion, cheese, salt, pepper and grated cheese to the mixture. Mix thoroughly with a fork.
4. Heat 2 TB oil in a large frying pan over medium/high heat.
5. Use a 1/3 cup measure to scoop batter onto the pan. Flatten the cakes slightly. Cook until browned and slightly crispy, 2-3 minutes. Flip over and brown the other side.
6. Add 1 TB more oil if necessary after the first 2 batches. Let the oil re-heat for a minute before making more pancakes.
7. Put the cooked pancakes on a plate lined with paper towels and keep warm in a 200-250° oven. You will have about 4 batches of pancakes, depending on how large you make them.
8. Serve as soon as they're all cooked, with garnishes of your choice.

Sides:
- Tossed green salad, or chopped vegetable salad
- Roasted broccoli or Brussels sprouts
- For hot weather, summer fruit salad or berries
- Deviled eggs (for non-vegans)
- Bacon or sausage (for meat eaters)

Nutty Waffles

Waffles for dinner? Waffles, or pancakes, make a nice change, and are great for quick cold weather dinners. Adding nuts boosts the protein. The recipe calls for hazelnuts, but you can use the same amount of pecans or 2/3 cup finely ground almond meal . Oily nuts like walnuts, or strong-flavored nuts like cashews wouldn't work so well.

Increase protein in the meal by topping the waffles with yogurt and serving milk as a beverage.

If you're used to drowning waffles and pancakes in syrup, you may need to re-think that if you're watching calories and added sugars. Some teens can stand the extra calories occasionally if they're active in sports and not overweight. Instead of syrup, try some of the topping suggestions below for variety. Or just eat them plain and enjoy the nutty flavor.

Note that this recipe is not vegan. Waffles depend on eggs for texture, so making waffles without real eggs will not work well.

Ingredients for about large 10 waffles
- 1 cup toasted hazelnuts or pecans
- 2-1/2 cups flour (you can substitute up to 1 cup whole wheat flour for white)
- 1 TB baking powder
- ½ tsp. baking soda
- ½ tsp. salt
- 2 cups buttermilk or 1 cup plus 1 cup low fat plain yogurt (not Greek style)
- ¼ cup canola oil
- 4 eggs
- optional: 1-1/2 tsp. vanilla extract

Toppings
Plain or flavored yogurt
fresh berries
sliced fresh fruit
shredded coconut
For an non-sweet unusual taste, try melting grated cheddar
cheese on the waffles. Goes great with sliced pears or apples.

290 calories • 9 gr protein • 16 gr fat • 29 g carbs • 2 gr fiber

Make the waffles

1. Whisk the dry ingredients together in a large bowl.
2. Pulse the hazelnuts or pecans in a food processor to a coarse fine texture and whisk into the flour mixture.
3. Whisk the eggs, buttermilk/yogurt and oil in a separate bowl.
4. Gently mix the liquid ingredients into the dry. Do not beat. Just stir to combine, leaving some small lumps.
5. Let the batter sit for a few minutes while you heat the waffle iron.
6. Cook the waffles according to waffle iron instructions to desired doneness. If not serving immediately, keep cooked waffles in a warm oven.

Sides:
- fresh fruit
- carrot cabbage coleslaw
- crunchy raw vegetable sticks
- bacon or cooked sausage for meat eaters; meatless versions for vegetarians and vegans

NO TIME TO COOK!

Sometimes cooking isn't an option. You have to get some kind of dinner on the table. Here are some fast, last minute fuss-free ideas using common foods.

1. **Frozen or take out cheese pizza** (not for vegans): order a veggie pizza, let meat eaters add their own meat (pepperoni, sausage, ground meat, chicken). Or forget the meat; just add vegetables like mushrooms, peppers, fresh tomato slices, sautéed onion or zucchini or eggplant, etc. Add a tossed salad or raw veggie sticks.

2. **Canned or take-out soup with bread and cheese.** This one is really easy. Vegans can add some canned beans to the soup, or have a nut butter or hummus instead of cheese. Add some sliced fruit for flavor contrast.

3. **Grilled sandwiches with chopped veggie salad:** Vegetarians can have grilled cheese. Vegans can try grilled nut butter or hummus sandwiches, and add eggplant, portabella mushrooms, fresh tomatoes or other veggies. Add some toasted pecans or almonds to the salad for more protein. Meat eaters can add leftover cooked chicken or turkey.

4. **Burritos or wraps:** easy for everyone. Prepare a variety of fillings, including ground meat, sautéed vegetables, refried beans, grated cheese, salsa, guacamole, hummus and chopped fresh tomatoes. For more protein, use Greek style plain yogurt instead of sour cream. Sautéed tofu chunks are another great option for vegans or vegetarians.

5. **Quiche:** This classic egg-based pie is off limits for vegans, but works great for vegetarians. Traditionally made with bacon and cream, it's easily adapted to a milk/egg/cheese recipe. Add sautéed vegetables: onions, broccoli, greens, peppers.

6. **Omelets:** As with quiche, omelets are not for vegans. Added bonus: they're quicker than baking a quiche.

7. **When you just want roast chicken or grilled steak:** If your meat entrée is accompanied by sides like salad, vegetables, potatoes, etc., and your teen vegetarian/vegan is a milk drinker (cow or soy), he or she can just eat the side dishes and drink milk to boost the protein in the meal.

8. **Mac and Cheese mix:** (not for vegans) Prepare boxed mac and cheese. Add sides like tossed salad, steamed or sautéed vegetables, raw vegetable sticks or fruit salad for balance.

SUMMING IT UP

Moving away from a meat-heavy diet, towards a more plant-based cuisine is a good plan for everyone. Whether your teen is making a long-term commitment to a vegetarian or vegan lifestyle, or is just experimenting with meatless cuisine for a few months, your family can use this as an opportunity to experiment with changes that are both healthful and timely.

Here's what I hope you got from this book:

1. A good basic understanding of vegetarian or vegan teen nutrition. Hopefully that information has given you some peace of mind about your teen's health. Additionally, you can recognize signs that suggest your teen's experiment with a vegetarian diet is becoming overly restrictive or turning into disordered eating.

2. Useful information on the potential health and environmental benefits of eating less meat. It's a good idea for everyone to eat less meat, so let this be an opportunity for the whole family to learn about plant-based meals.

3. A variety of basic recipes to get you going. Remember, your teen needs to be involved with this process, thinking about protein foods, picking recipes, taste-testing new ingredients. This should not turn into yet another chore for Mom or Dad.

Other Resources

This book is just the beginning of the journey. There are plenty of other resources for recipes and tips on new food products and meatless menus. Here are a few:

Meatless Monday website
MeatlessMonday.com

Oldways Preservation Trust Vegetarian Network
Oldwayspt.org

Vegetarian Resource Group
www.vrg.org

USDA Vegetarian Resource page
fnic.nal.usda.gov/lifecycle-nutrition/vegetarian-nutrition

Academy of Nutrition and Dietetics vegetarian teen resources
www.eatright.org/resource/food/nutrition/vegetarian-and-special-diets/menu-ideas-for-vegetarian-teens

Soy Foods Council
www.soyfoods.org

Whole Grains Council
Wholegrainscouncil.org

Look for tips on the *Feed Your Vegetarian Teen* Website and Feed Your Vegetarian Teen Facebook page. You can ask questions or submit your own ideas, success stories and product tips. You can also check out my blog at Radio Nutrition for more tips on nutrition in general.

References

Chapter 1

Scientific Report of the 2015 Dietary Guidelines Advisory Committee. www.health.gov/dietaryguidelines/2015-scientific-report/04-integration.asp

"Primary Prevention of Cardiovascular Disease." New England Journal of Medicine 2013; 368:1279-1290

"Red meat consumption and risk of Type 2 diabetes." American Journal of Clinical Nutrition 2011 ajcn.018978

"Beyond Meatless: the health effects of vegan diets." Nutrients 2014, 6(6), 2131-2147

"Vegetarian diets and blood pressure." Journal of the American Medical Association Internal Medicine. 2014;174(4):577-58

"Predominantly Plant Diets Help Patients Shed Pounds" MedPage Today. www.medpagetoday.com/MeetingCoverage/ObesityWeek/42944

"Major Habitual Dietary patterns are associated with acute myocardial infarction and cardiovascular risk markers in a southern European population" J.Am.Diet.Assoc. 2011;111:241-250

"Nutrient Profiles of Vegetarian and Nonvegetarian Dietary Patterns" J Acad Nutr Diet. 2013;113:1610-1619

Chapter 2

"In U.S. 5% consider themselves vegetarians" Gallup survey.
www.gallup.com/poll/156215/Consider-Themselves-Vegetarians.aspx

Eating Disorder Referral and Information Center:
www.edreferral.com

The Eating Disorder Foundation:
www.eatingdisorderfoundation.com

National Eating Disorders Association:
www.nationaleatingdisorders.org

U.S. Grocery Shopper Trends 2015 Food Marketing Institute Food
Marketing Institute www.fmioorg/research-resources/u-s-grocery-
shopper-trends-2015

Chapter 3

"Protein and Amino Acids" Dietary Reference Intakes. Chapter 10.
National Academies Press 2005
www.nap.edu/openbook.php?record_id=10490&page=589

"Protein Digestibility Corrected Amino Acid Score" Wikipedia
en.wikipedia.org/wiki/Protein_Digestibility_Corrected_Amino_Acid_
Score

"FAO report on dietary protein quality evaluation in human
nutrition" British Nutrition Foundation.
www.nutrition.org.uk/nutritioninthenews/new-reports/faoprotein

Nutraingredients June 20, 2014.
www.nutraingredients.com/Regulation-Policy/Five-years-reasonable-
time-frame-for-FAO-DIAAS-adoption-Volac

Diet for a Small Planet by Frances Moore Lappé.
Smallplanet.org/books

Centers for Disease Control. Nutrition for Everyone: Protein.
www.cdc.gov/nutrition/everyone/basics/protein.html

The 2015 US Dietary Guidelines: Lifting the Ban on Total Dietary Fat.
Darriush Mozaffarian, MD DrPH and David Ludwig MD PhD. JAMA
313(24)2421-2

Chapter 5

Nature. Dec 2, 2013. Humans are becoming more carnivorous.
www.nature.com/news/humans-are-becoming-more-carnivorous-
1.14282

"Feed the World" National Geographic Magazine.
www.nationalgeographic.com/foodfeatures/feeding-9-billion/

United Nations Food and Agriculture Organization issue paper:
Energy-Smart Food for people and climate. 2011.
www.fao.org/docrep/014/i2454e/i2454e00.pdf

National Geographic Magazine
http://environment.nationalgeographic.com/environment/global-
warming/end-cheap-oil/

Am J Clin Nutr September 2003 vol. 78 no. 3 660S-663S.
"Sustainability of meat-based and plant-based diets and the
environment." by David and Marcia Pimentel.
http://ajcn.nutrition.org/content/78/3/660S.abstract

Food, Energy and Society, Third Edition. By David and Marcia
Pimentel. CRC Press 2007.

Journal of Health Services Research & Policy 20(1)39-44
http://hsr.sagepub.com/content/20/1/39.full.pdf

National Geographic Magazine
http://ngm.nationalgeographic.com/2007/04/global-fisheries-crisis/did-
you-know-learn

"The End of the Line" by Bryan Walsh. Time Magazine July 7, 2011. http://content.time.com/time/health/article/0,8599,2081796-1,00.html

"Fish Farming's Growing Dangers" by Ken Stier. Time Magazine Sept 19, 2007. http://content.time.com/time/health/article/0,8599,1663604,00.html

"How to Farm a Better Fish" National Geographic Magazine http://www.nationalgeographic.com/foodfeatures/aquaculture/

The Nature Conservancy. The Water Footprint of an American. http://www.nature.org/ourinitiatives/habitats/riverslakes/explore/water-footprint-of-an-american.xml?src=e.nature

National Bison Association. www.bisoncentral.com

"Diet change – a solution to reduce water use?" M Jalava *et al* 2014 *Environ. Res. Lett.* **9** 074016. http://iopscience.iop.org/1748-9326/9/7/074016/

The Water Footprint Network. http://www.waterfootprint.org/?page=cal/WaterFootprintCalculator

Additional reading: "Carnivore's Dilemma." National Geographic Magazine. November 2014: 109-135.

Recipe Index

A - B

Barley with Greens and Beans	76
Bean Burgers, vegan black bean	48
Bean Burgers, vegetarian	43
Black bean salad	52
Black bean stuffed sweet potatoes	114
Buckwheat (soba) noodles	94

C - D

Cassoulet	60
Cheese potato bake	110
Chili	58
Couscous, Mediterranean	96
Dal (Curried Lentils)	62

G - N

Garbanzo beans, sautéed	66
Mediterranean couscous	96
Minestrone (bean vegetable soup)	54
Mukimame Salad	68
Nutty Waffles	120

P - Q

Pad Thai-style Rice Noodles	100
Pasta Salad	106
Polenta Pizza	82
Potato Pancakes	118
Pumped Up Ramen	104
Quinoa Summer Salad	88

R - S

Rice with Cashews and Coconut	72
Risotto	78
Soba Noodles	94
Stuffed Baked Potatoes	112
Sweet Potato Chili	117
Sweet Potatoes, Black bean stuffed	114

T - Z

Tabouli	90
Unfried Rice	86
Vegetable Pasta Variations	102
Vegetarian Bean Burgers	43
Waffles, nutty	120

ABOUT THE AUTHOR

Donna P Feldman, MS RDN, holds a Masters Degree in Nutrition and Communications from Cornell University. She's been a Registered Dietitian Nutritionist for more than 35 years.

Her interest in nutrition evolved over many years. She experimented with vegetarian cooking while still in college, and ran one of the first vegetarian cafeteria lines at Williams College in Massachusetts. Since then, she's worked in nutrition research, patient counseling, college instruction, media, software design and food service management. For several years she ran a personal chef business specializing in calorie-controlled healthy meals. She currently blogs about food, diets and nutrition on her Radio Nutrition website, and is co-host of the *Walk Talk Nutrition* podcast series.

Made in the USA
Las Vegas, NV
17 December 2021

38361165R00079